THE
QUANTUM KEY

Transcending Life's Trials

Tonya Zavasta

Beautiful On Raw, Inc

The Quantum Key: Transcending Life's Trials

Published by BEAUTIFUL ON RAW, INC.
P.O. Box 276, Orangevale, California 95662

ISBN 978-0-9742434-8-1

Cover design: Dan Denysenko, Vladimir Volegov, Alexey Chernovalov
Editors: Bradley Harris, Joel Brody
Proofreading by Richard L. Sine
Photography by Serge Balenko
Layout by Yev Denysenko, Alexey Chernovalov

Publisher's Cataloging-in-Publication
(Provided by Quality Books, Inc.)

Zavasta, Tonya, author.
    The quantum key : transcending life's trials / Tonya Zavasta.
    pages cm
    LCCN 2015920705
    ISBN 978-0-9742434-8-1

    1. Self-actualization (Psychology) 2. Success--Psychological aspects.   I. Title.

BF637.S4Z38 2016   158.1
                          QBI15-600232

Printed in Canada

Table of Contents

Introduction

This email came in response to an initial newsletter announcement about this book. The working title was *The Quantum Key: Solving Life's Problems…*

Why not give the book's subtitle a more positive spin? Instead of focusing on "life's problems," how about the phrase "revolutionary lifestyle"? Or perhaps this title: "Radical Solutions to Anti – Aging"?

Thoughtful, plausible suggestions. I can see how my previous books have influenced her. She's read them, and now holds reasonable expectations. I appreciate that!

With this new book, I'm *defying* expectations. This new venture is definitely not just another book about healthful eating. Nor is it focused on "radical solutions to anti-aging," or on the kind of "revolutionary lifestyle" you'd expect from a raw foods advocate. No blueberries, broccoli, or beauty sleep here.

Still, the email got me thinking. We're conditioned to think about that word *problem* as naming something that's inherently negative. To be sure, the word *problem*, in one definition, does carry a distinctly negative flavor. Tribulation, hardship — a situation "regarded as harmful and needing to be overcome," as one dictionary puts it.

A mathematician by education, I couldn't help seeing some mathematical parallels. Is a math problem a *negative* thing? Is a research problem somehow a detriment? Of course not! Let's allow another definition to kick in to define that old word *problem*: an inquiry, starting from conditions we're handed, and moving through investigation toward demonstration of some fact, result, or law.

The day I started seeing every "problem" in this light was my turning point. I did change the book's subtitle. You would agree, the word *trial* looks better on the cover. It carries just a snippet of salt, perhaps of pain. But it also brings to mind the notion of *trying* or *testing,* so it better reflects what the book is all about.

Throughout my writings, I use the word *problem* with that second definition in mind. In math, you always move forward after solving a problem. The very same thing happens in dealing with life's challenges.

A trial in life is a signpost to a better you, *if* you follow it. You'll have to go somewhere you've never been before. Sure, you'll have to put out some effort. But in the end, you have been led to something valuable. You've learned something new. You have grown.

There are two parts to every locking system: the lock itself and its matching key. The metaphor is: The solution is always a part of the problem. Even where there's no easy, obvious key, you'll find the most organic, most effective solution somewhere within the problem itself, amid the conditions that created the problem in the first place.

We're going to use problems to find solutions. That means looking not *at* the problem, but *through* it. Seeing how the problem works, and why it's there.

This is not a book about "conquering" problems. It's about transcending them. Going beyond them. And, always, mining the difficulties of our lives for the treasures they contain.

After reading this book, I hope you'll never again think

about your "problems" as your adversaries. They are, in truth, your allies.

Everything in this book I have tried myself, transcending some of my most challenging life's trials. Let me start with my own childhood condition.

Gale's Encyclopedia of Children's Health says: Unless corrected soon after birth, congenital hip dysplasia (CHD) can cause a characteristic limp or waddling gait in children. If left untreated, the child will have difficulty walking and may experience life-long pain...

Some medical conditions are as bad as they sound. CHD is one of those. My problem was not "corrected soon after birth." Hospital stays and endless surgeries consumed my childhood. Pain, most likely to be permanent, was my reality.

Orthopedists warned that untreated hip dysplasia would lead to arthritis and debilitating deterioration of my hip. They were right. I limped for fifty years. My entire body, head to toe, suffered misalignment from trying to compensate for my damaged right hip.

At 42, I had both hips replaced. There were complications. My orthopedic doctors told me I'd be wheelchair-bound for life. (On the positive side, I would always get great parking spaces.)

The doctors weren't right about everything. Today, at 58, I have no trace of my once-pronounced limp. No crookedness. And there's no wheelchair or walker hidden in my closet, waiting. Instead, I now have a graceful body, with the proportions and the flexibility of an 18 year-old!

Does it sound like I'm bragging here? Like I'm typing this while wearing my Wonder Woman costume? (Note to self:

Check eBay for one of those.) Maybe there is a little hubris here. But give me a break, won't you? I want to encourage you, so that you, too, can solve your problems, no matter how impossible they may seem now.

Do you, for example, have marital or relationship problems? So did I. Soon after the wedding, I understood why marriage is called *wedlock*. For the first sixteen years, I felt locked in an unhappy union. Today, I'm blessed with a loving, caring, supportive husband. And guess what? He's the same guy.

Are you struggling financially? I know how you feel. In 1991, when we first immigrated to the USA, we had to literally count pennies to make it, one day to the next. Now I have my own beauty company. The products I've created are used in more than 50 countries. I've written eight books, even though English is my second language, and have thousands of loyal readers around the world. (My thanks go to everyone of you.)

After years of bouncing from one of life's challenges to the next, my discovery that you can solve *all* your problems was quite a revelation. I just wish I'd seen it sooner.

You *can* solve *all* your problems. I really like that phrase. I used it in drafting an article once, but my editor had the audacity to remove it, dang him! The word *all* bugged him, I suspect. Exaggeration, he likely thought.

But perhaps you, too, think this line — *You can solve all your problems* — is presumptuous, if not downright preposterous.

What about the person with late-stage cancer that doctors have pronounced terminal, or someone sentenced to life in prison without parole? No solutions, right?

Our robust sense of reality does compel us to admit some

solutions are beyond the frontier of the possible, and deep into the impossible. But is there a definite line between the two? Patients sentenced to death by disease do get healed. The imprisoned do get pardoned. Not every day perhaps, but often enough for us to hear of such cases.

That's the purpose of this book — to explore what makes the difference, what helps find the answer in difficult, even desperate straits.

Dealing with my life's problems, I've learned a lot. Now I believe I can help *you* find extraordinary solutions to *your* challenges.

Too much "I" here? I — Oops! Here it is again — felt that way in writing this chapter, racking up my accomplishments. But how could I say I did this or that, yet also convey that it wasn't some separate, disconnected, ego-centered *I* that solved those problems?

Language is where the trouble lies. Those pronouns — *I, you, he, she, my, them* — imply distinction, difference, distance. Truth is, I had a lot of help dealing with those trials. (Just as you could have.) All that *I* notwithstanding, this book is about *you*. It's about *us*. It's about how we can all enlist the help we need to become happy, fulfilled, and free.

CHAPTER 1

Change Your Beliefs, Change Your Life!

M y grandaunt Maria loved to sing the hymn with the words: *And I long to be by my Savior's side, Just over in the glory land.* She died at age 85.

During her last days, she'd express over and over how much she didn't want to die, how she wished she could live just a little longer. She was decrepit, could barely see, and was always complaining of aches and pains. And I thought, "How could such an existence possibly be better than the *'glory land?'*" This question has bothered me since childhood.

One biblical verse has become a revelation to me: *Remember your leaders, who spoke the word of God to you. Consider the outcome of their way of life, and imitate their faith.* (Hebrews 13:7). Another translation states it this way: *Bear in mind how they ended their lives, and imitate their faith.*

The message I got from it is: the best way to test any belief someone holds is to observe how it has affected his way of life, and especially at the time of his death. That's exactly what I like to do, applying the principle to the living and to those who've passed away.

People interest me. I love to analyze a person's life and see how his or her beliefs have framed it. Whose lives have inspired you? Most importantly, would you like to live the rest of your life like them? To die like them? If yes, their belief systems are well worth examining.

A thorough review of your own life and even a casual look at the lives of others will convince you that what shapes a person's life is his or her belief system.

We are what we believe. Many of these beliefs were formed during our childhood. We were influenced by our parents, teachers, and friends, as well as where we lived and grew up.

Our parents' beliefs usually became our beliefs. We were raised in our parents' religion, or its absence. In the same way, our political beliefs are often shaped at home, whether we're Republican or Democrat, Conservative or Labor, Utopian or Anarchist.

Some of us were brought up on steak and potatoes for dinner, while others have never eaten anything with fuzz or a face. Still others were left to their own devices, and were brought up with a TV, a tray, a frozen dinner and a box of Tater Tots.

Are your beliefs right or wrong? It's not my place to say.

I can talk properly only about my own. Living in the former Soviet Union, my mother was a member of the Communist party, and as a youth, I earnestly shared her beliefs. Then I learned that we, like millions of others, were deceived. That was a life-changing—no, life-*shattering*—experience.

It was then I resolved I would never accept *any* idea—especially, any *system* of ideas—without investigating it from every possible angle. When I realized my mom's political position was flawed, I began looking critically at all other aspects of my life: how I was living and what I was thinking.

We rarely, if ever, question the belief systems at the bosom of which we were raised. If you're a Republican or Democrat "because Daddy was," that's quite a flimsy reason. Likewise, if your religious affiliation is based on the simple fact that this is what you've "always believed," I invite you to ask yourself: *From where did that belief come? On whose authority does my belief rest? How did it develop? What alternatives may be out there?*

Ever find yourself all bent and twisted because your cherished beliefs feel threatened? You may have raised your voice, got crabby in an email, or started talking in snappish tones, *"Now, look here!"* Maybe you've even hurled a few angry words at someone.

Consider this: your charged emotion just might flag a weakness in your belief system. It could signal that what you've believed all along is not aligned with the truth.

My friend Scott, upon reading these lines above, asked me: *Do you mean that if I don't have strong arguments to justify my belief, and I get emotional, my belief is wrong?*

The fact that you can't explain why you've held one belief or another all your life doesn't make it wrong. But it does mean you've inherited this belief blindly—most likely from your parents or someone else in authority.

You picked up this belief not through your own research or reasoning, but by it simply—even unconsciously—being passed on to you. It also reveals that you have never since subjected your belief to a critical analysis. Still, the emotional uprising alone doesn't make your belief wrong.

However, keep in mind that getting frustrated or furious when your unexamined belief is challenged does border dangerously on an uncritical obsession, called fanaticism.

All of this begs the question: *What about faith? Faith is also a belief that is not based on proof.* Let me answer it by answering another question: What's the difference between faith and fanaticism? There is *a world of difference.*

A person who holds faith based on truth always has an indirect knowledge of that truth, if only intuitively. Even if he cannot explain his faith in words, he'll always exhibit it in his behavior.

Faith based on truth leads to great confidence, calmness, and inner serenity. A person of such faith doesn't get annoyed or irritated when his belief is challenged. He is so secure that he won't lash out verbally or emotionally at his opponent, but will listen calmly and compassionately as his companion presents her arguments.

Faith is about doing. You are how you act, not just how you believe.

— Mitch Albom

14

Fanaticism, on the other hand, makes a person insecure. The fanatic hides his lack of confidence behind emotion, refusing to hear any rational argument.

Truth never needs to be defended. It's big. It's powerful. It's universal. It supports you. It doesn't need to be supported by you.

"The unexamined life is not worth living," Socrates advised us long ago. It's no less true that the unexamined, unchallenged position is not worth holding. Give your own beliefs the same careful consideration you'd like others to give. And study others' viewpoints with the same kind of care, respect, and thought you'd like directed at your own.

A willingness to analyze beliefs as new information comes to light is important to the wellbeing of an individual, and to humanity as a whole. The more certain we are of our rightness, the more critically we need to examine other viewpoints through reading and study.

I'm interested in exploring the kinds of belief that offer real joy in daily life and, especially, nearing death. Not the sort of temporary, private joy you might find in humming a favorite hymn, but the kind you can *see* outright in a person's countenance day to day—a joy so obvious that words are unnecessary. *That's* the belief I want to emulate!

The art of living well and the art of dying well are one.

— Epicurus

15

I became fascinated with accounts of people who died joyously, and, in the process, I found some profound answers on how I might *live* joyously. Am I leaping about gleefully 24/7? No — I'm happy, not nuts! I've had my share of setbacks and disappointments, and I certainly harbor my own restricting beliefs. But over the last eighteen years, the slope of my life on the joy scale has definitely been *upward*.

Most of us don't like the prospect of having our beliefs changed, even challenged. I was the same way until I realized some of my beliefs were keeping me from seeing solutions to present problems, even inviting new problems into my life. Each time life wanted me to follow a new path, here was a boulder to trip over, some obstacle my own beliefs were setting before me.

How do we decide which beliefs we should keep and which to let go? By answering the following questions with a resounding "Yes!" Does *acting* on those beliefs feel totally right to us? Do these beliefs bring progressively more joy, month after month, year after year, giving all signs of reaching a *crescendo* at the time of our departure from this earth?

Our belief systems form a sort of encasement, a box. It may even become more like a prison. Our most dearly held beliefs mark our most sacred boundaries. But problems that arise in life often cannot be solved as long as we continue to stay steadfast within the borders of our acquired beliefs.

Let us begin with the critical examination of the traditions, habits, and beliefs with which you were raised, and those you acquired later, but still hold dear and true.

All of our problems, including health, relationships, and

money, often have surprising solutions.

Just because something is tradition doesn't make it right.

— Anthony J. D'Angelo

Eating what you've always eaten might not be the right way to keep you free of disease. Praying the way you've always prayed might not be the right way to receive answers. And, thinking the way you've always thought might not be the right way to live, free of worries and fears, including the fear of death.

The perfect reason we should seek the truth is that the truth is *good* for us. It's truth which permits you to find solutions to all your challenges. Even a glimpse of truth leads to more truth, just as a glimpse of light leads to more light.

The truth must be reached at all costs if you want to reach a solution to your problem, no matter how unpopular that truth may be.

How much truth can you take without running back to the fortress of your beliefs? That will determine how thoroughly, how soon, how easily you can transform your life. The seeker of truth must be willing to listen, willing to learn something new, willing even to accommodate new truths which do violence to old beliefs.

Let me borrow a metaphor from the mid-twentieth century philosophical giant Ludwig Wittgenstein: Each of us is like a fly inside a glass bottle. We never seem to see that narrow opening at the top. Whichever way we go, we keep hitting the invisible glass that separates us from the real world. That glass is like our belief system, limiting and trapping us.

In the following chapters, I endeavor to show that we don't have to struggle, that the way out of the bottle is actually easy and totally satisfying. Would you like to become healthier, happier, and more fulfilled with each passing year? Then get ready to have some of your most cherished beliefs seriously ruffled.

CHAPTER 2

Don't Follow the Herd!

My friend Scott wrote that he wanted three experts to give this book a pre-publication review: *a Methodist preacher, a retired Ph.D. physicist, and the head of the Theology and Philosophy Department at a prestigious university.*

I did give Scott's well-intentioned suggestion careful consideration.

It's amazing, really — how deeply we've absorbed the notion that we must seek the approval of some "establishment" or other, always looking side to side, making sure we're in line with all the experts. Let us examine this belief.

If the real answer to your problem were available from the mainstream via the usual routes, then wouldn't you already know it? And would your problem still be there?

Thomas Kuhn describes two kinds of science in his book, *The Structure of Scientific Revolutions.* "Normal" science, says Kuhn, supports existing theories. "Extraordinary" science happens, however, when investigators begin to consider those unsolved problems often dismissed as unsolvable by "normal" science. These riskier research ventures will often create wholly new paradigms of thought.

Reading the history of science, Thomas Kuhn observed: It takes a long time for a revolutionary idea to reach the mainstream. And by the time it does, it's no longer good enough because there's already something better.

Many of the most helpful methods I've found are controversial. They do not, typically, receive the *Good Housekeeping* Seal of Approval or the blessings of the mainstream scientific establishment.

Pain, addiction, depression, relationship issues, and a host of other human problems, all point to this conclusion: Many of our paradigms aren't working anymore. What it will take to solve life's problems goes beyond mere "adjustment" in our thinking about rules and standards in several fields — health, nutrition, culture, religion, and societal norms. No — what we need is a full-blast demolition of old standards and structures, to be supplanted with fresh new ideas — often ideas diametrically opposed to the old ones.

To solve our life's problems, we need to break free from the herd mentality. I like the line from the film of David Mamet's *Glengarry Glen Ross:* "I subscribe to the law of contrary public opinion ... If everyone thinks one thing, then I say, bet the other way..."

Now, there's a logical fallacy buried in there. That "everyone" believes something *isn't* evidence that it's false. And if an idea falls outside the mainstream, that alone doesn't count as evidence that it's true. Nonetheless, we have a lot more to learn from the exceptions to popular beliefs than from simply following what "everyone knows." Popular wisdom counts for nothing by itself.

You don't have to take my word for it. The best minds throughout history have said the same thing. Pythagoras warned, "Do not take roads traveled by the public... that which happens to the multitude is absurd and ridiculous." He instructed his students not to follow the roads of the masses, but the roads of the few. Good advice 2,600 years ago. Good advice now.

The minority is sometimes right: the majority always wrong.

— George Bernard Shaw

We're often victimized by what the crowd—"society"—wants, or says, or even insists upon. And advertising, the ultimate influencer of herd mentality, sways us time and again.

For instance, a typical Westerner eats a pizza, or a steak sandwich, or some other highly processed item advertised on TV. Soon, he'll be wondering how he gained all that weight, why he feels sick and sluggish, how he got arthritis, acid reflux, or diabetes. By the time he's in his sixties, he'll down a saucer of pills a day that he saw advertised on TV. He sits on a couch and zones out on the unreality of reality TV. In another decade, he'll shuffle off this mortal coil, full of regret and guilt. Our friend Pythagoras would say, and we'd have to agree: *It's all rather absurd.*

I can hear some voices out there... *Yo! Tonya! What business do you have criticizing me?*

But I am not. That uneasiness that you felt comes not from outside, not from me — I just tossed out some facts. That uncomfortable feeling comes from within, from your own knowledge that you cannot go on with the life you're leading now. And I'm here only to help.

My life began to improve dramatically only when I started to question what the majority believed. Often, I found real gems in unique, long — neglected, sometimes outright frowned-upon beliefs and practices. These days, I find myself holding a fair number of views not shared by the majority. And I'm far better off for it.

Our medical and nutritional sciences are, for example, still in the stage of "normal science." But more and better doctors conventionally trained... more drugs... early diagnosis... more store-shelf "natural" supplements — stack these up as high as you like — are still not going to solve our big health crisis. *People* are sick, because the *paradigm* is sick.

Society offers Band-Aid solutions. Quick fixes. *Here, take a pill!* Treat the symptoms, not the cause. You won't solve the problem, but you may conceal it for a while.

The best, most original answers to problems often don't come from where you'd expect. They don't spring from conventional sources. They're not associated with university endorsements. No — those best solutions often come from "outside," from paradigm-shifting ideas that offer new perspectives on familiar facts that question commonly agreed upon fundamentals.

To find a solution, *stop* doing what everyone else does.

Stop being so easily, so automatically, led by "experts." Don't worship at the idol of conformity. When authorities foist grandly pronounced answers to life's problems upon you, go find your own solutions.

It's never easy to go against the social grain, to stand out and purposefully make yourself different. Still, we must. Whatever your goal — superior health, longevity, financial security, relationship harmony, or even access to heaven — independent thinking is the way. It's time — high time — to begin questioning. Questioning what? Well, *everything*.

Truth doesn't lie about on the surface, like a volleyball lying on a beach, waiting for you to seize it. Truth waits to be dug for. Self-education is part of that digging.

Research everything. Read different authors. Read what's unfashionable, flaky, edgy, not-quite-doctor-approved. Remain free from prejudice, from unexamined public opinion. Question the mainstream authors. Question the "outsider" authors no less.

One day at a time, you'll gain a different prospective. You'll be undermining old, stale beliefs that have been holding you back for years.

You degree-holders, beware: It's often in our own fields of expertise that we may find the biggest pile of biases, unspoken assumptions, triggers, and hedge-barriers that prevent us from solving our problems.

So many experts, so many opinions, whom to believe? I've adopted this standard: I listen to everyone who gives advice, but I mostly seek to learn from those who have achieved what I want to have.

Few of the ideas I present here have come from "professors" or anyone else of that ilk. Instead, I've learned most from the people we might call *masters* — people who have achieved real results in every aspect of a fulfilled and happy life.

I learn health from people who are beaming with health. I learn spirituality from people who practice love and gratitude every moment of their lives. And I learn philosophy from those rare individuals who have long forgotten how fear and life's problems can drag them down.

Opinions of the masses kill the 'extra' in an 'extraordinary' idea.

— Mokokoma Mokhonoana

The formula for ordinary: Stick with the other sheep in the herd. The formula for extraordinary: Well, there *isn't* one, which is part of my point. But if there were a recipe for becoming extraordinary, achieving the extraordinary, it would begin with this one step: Break away from the herd.

Thankful as I am for Scott's idea, I'm not getting this book peer-reviewed. I'm not "doing physics." Not starting a new religion. This book is about my life, and what I've learned experimenting with the ideas rather removed from "normal" science, with the ideas some accomplished stragglers from the herd found to be quite extraordinary.

CHAPTER 3

On Becoming Quantum-Friendly

T*he Quantum Key?* Why that title? Physics? What's that got to do with our lives, or anything?

Truth is, quantum theory has *everything* to do with *everything*. Including, as it happens, with our bodies, our minds, and beyond. What better basis for a book? And what better reason to learn a little about quantum physics?

It's not just a theory *in* physics — it has by now come into its own as the very basis *of* physics. It's the foundation of nearly every derivative subject from chemistry to cosmetology.

Quantum theory impacts much of our economy. Laser technology, for example, directly depends on quantum theory and wouldn't exist without it. If you're reading an e-version of this page, the microprocessor it's running on is a product of quantum theory. Electronics of all kinds owe their advancements to quantum physics. And wait until you see what's coming next!

Quantum. The word might suggest to some readers that

quirky, complicated, super-mathematical stuff that's really understood only by twelve scientific geeks around the whole world. That reminds me...

A word on the side to you physics specialists, whether you're a professor or just a buff. All my references to quantum physics aren't about *physics*. I'll leave that to you guys. Rather, I'm speaking about *interpretations* of quantum mechanics that can profoundly improve our lives.

Since my aim is to make quantum-mechanical concepts widely comprehensible, the explanations I present here will not endure scientific scrutiny. My book is practical. It *can* help you resolve your life's problems, but for Tuesday morning's physics exam, you'll need to look elsewhere!

For those of you who'd prefer that I don't mention any theoretical physics, I'd say: Resist the urge to skip even a single paragraph in the next chapter. I'll make it as painless as possible. Read as if your life depends on it. *Because it does.*

Even though it may not seem like it, solutions to our problems are always present, always *somewhere* within our grasp. Consider the concept of *opposites*. It reveals itself everywhere. We see it in the physical realm: light and dark, day and night, front and back. Opposites are an essential aspect of life and biology: male and female, life and death, organic and inorganic.

Name anything, and it'll have an opposite—like problems and solutions. You can't have one without the other. Why don't we see solutions so readily then?

Because our old mental model of reality, not the reality

itself, determines how many options we'll see. The answers surround us, but our established beliefs block the view, beliefs that we've carried around for years, like worn-out baggage.

How you view reality directly affects how you see your own abilities to take control of it. Know that just by reading about the discoveries of quantum physics, and trying to make sense of them, you've already started on improving your life.

One discovery in quantum physics — and a key one in this book, as you'll learn: Particles, "things," change their properties as a consequence of their being observed. The observer, if you will, changes the event.

It does appear that quantum physics puts forth the idea that our minds create our own reality. If there were even the smallest chance this is true, would you want to remain ignorant to the possibility?

Another discovery we'll use is quantum entanglement. But entangled *what*? Particles, to be exact. It appears that the state of one particle *here* can influence the state of another particle over *there* — the other side of the room, or the other side of the galaxy. What's more, it seems that influence can happen *instantaneously*, much faster, indeed, than the speed of light.

And, speaking of light, it's the new electricity. Since the advent of the transistor radio, developments in practical electronics have been all about *making it smaller*.

We can expect within a decade, we're told, to see commonplace personal devices that use light itself in place of conventional electricity. They'll give us lightning-speed search engines, and stunningly fast communication of all kinds, with data-encryption that promises higher security than we've ever seen.

Your cell phone—if it's even to be called that—will be a marvel of speed, accuracy, and reliability, with vastly more capability than any computer you're now using.

The *quantum information* revolution is already underway.

By now, we're all familiar with the basic notion of how information is stored in computers. It's the idea of *bits*-ones and zeroes. It's a one-or-the-other thing. One. Or zero. Two choices. But, thanks to discoveries in quantum physics, it seems a particle can be in two states at the same time.

A classical computer switch offers one *and* zero. Quantum information is stored not in bits but in "qubits," whose value can be one or zero, but can also be both zero and one at the same time.

Now imagine what a "quantum CD" would be like… It would offer *fantastic* potential, containing not only a particular song, but *all* the songs, even all *possible* songs—past, present, and future.

Quantum computing is to conventional computing as a nuclear bomb is to a firecracker. The world's fastest conventional computer (called "Q") has a footprint of *one full acre*. But just a few atoms of a quantum computer are able to perform computations that would require the power of so many "Q" computers that they'd cover the whole surface of the Earth.

In just minutes, a quantum computer will be able to solve mathematical conundrums that would take a classical computer a billion years!

Will all this happen in your lifetime? Most likely, yes. Science fiction is becoming science fact. IBM researchers claim they're now close to a technology that will allow them to build a "minimum" quantum computer. It might happen any day.

Maybe it already has, and you'll read about it tomorrow.

The quantum theory, which originated in 1900 when Max Planck first suggested that radiation was quantized, has been delivering technical marvels to us since the beginning of its long growing-up phase.

However, we shouldn't think the next gadget from Apple or Microsoft will be the best or most advanced device by which to judge quantum physics. The greatest value in quantum theory may lie in how it helps us think, how it helps us rethink the universe and our place within it.

The doctrine that the world is made up of objects whose existence is independent of human consciousness turns out to be in conflict with quantum mechanics and with facts established by experiment.

— Bernard d'Espagnat, French theoretical physicist and philosopher of science

---

We do still live in a material world. The familiar tree in the yard will still be there when you get up from reading this book. Newtonian apples will still fall from it in autumn. The billiard balls and dropped bricks of high school physics will continue to behave as they always have. The old Rutherford model of the atom — neutron, proton, electron — will still be a good way to explain the structure of an atom to a five-year-old, but what's *under* all of this has changed. Radically. And forever. That's the legacy of quantum theory.

To more fully, more meaningfully benefit from living in

today's world, it behooves us to move toward understanding the implications of quantum theory, not just for the natural sciences but also for our world, our lives, and our thoughts.

Quantum mechanics suggests that it's your observation, your participation, and even more so your *expectations* that "command" the quantum field to manifest into being concrete, distinct, material things, and states of affairs.

Many physicists, even eminent ones, avoid dealing with the whole issue of consciousness. Their pragmatic solution: Use quantum physics for the micro-world, and classical physics for the macro-world. Just ignore the implications that make you uncomfortable. But encounter consciousness they must. There is no way around it.

We "create" our own realities, although your basic physicist may well scoff at that notion. His objection: You can't apply theories and observations operating in the micro-world of subatomic particles and apply them to what you choose for lunch and how you'll achieve your dreams. To that I say *Okay* and shrug. In the end, if you can create a healthy, joyful, abundant life, would you really care if the standard physics texts didn't approve of how you did it?

The applications of quantum physics are changing our very way of life, solving practical problems from cell phones to air lasers, and so much more. It's time we start using quantum physics implications to solve our personal problems. I've become convinced that even a cursory look into quantum mechanics, applying its lessons in our daily life, is capable of changing our thinking and transforming our lives.

Physicists agree: quantum mechanics makes no sense, in conventional terms. But it *works* in all practical applications. A quantum computer will be making *unimaginable* computations. In much the same way, allowing your beliefs to become "quantum-friendly" will lift your life to unimaginable heights. The time has come to suspend your disbelief and challenge the notion of the impossible.

CHAPTER 4

Bigger World… More Options

*V*ibrations. Now there's a word that sets people twitching (which is in itself, come to think of it, a kind of vibration). If you feel uncomfortable when someone talks in terms of our thoughts, our bodies, our whole universe consisting of energy or electro-magnetic waves ("vibrations") of different frequencies, you're not alone.

Tough to grasp for most of us, which is understandable. But as soon as someone says, *Nonsense! This vibration business doesn't exist...* there's a problem. We owe it to ourselves to think more openly and more rationally than that.

One issue that bothers some people is that all this talk about "vibrations" isn't scientific. But it is. It's clear that quantum physics seconds what Pythagoras said some 2,500 years ago: "Our senses are deceitful. But they shall mislead mankind no more."

Well, they still do. Do you believe your senses—vision, hearing, smell, taste and touch—convey to you the true nature of reality? Now this is the belief that needs to be examined quite carefully. It's the mother of all false beliefs, the one that keeps generating problems for us.

So how *do* we see? Our retinas absorb light from outside and convey signals to the brain. A rose is not *inherently* red. Grass is not *in and of itself* green. But the surfaces of grass and rose petals are such that each reflects some colors and absorbs all the others. We perceive only the reflected colors. Color thus originates in *light* — in light waves — and not in the objects themselves.

Most of what's out there we can't see at all. And what we do see is not there. The rainbow represents one slice of the electromagnetic spectrum that our senses pick up. We're blind to the rest of the spectrum. And yet, a rainbow is an optical illusion.

A rainbow is always oriented dead-center to the observer's point of view, wherever that individual may be. You'll never see it from the side, or even from an angle. Like so many "things" in the world, the rainbow is constructed for us — and by us — via complex systems fed by data transmitted by our senses.

How do we hear? Sound waves enter the ear canal, reach the eardrum, and set it vibrating. The brain interprets these vibrations as sound.

Our mind has a lot to do with what we see and hear. How about the material objects around us? At least they have to be real, right? Not so fast. "Reality," said Einstein, "is merely an illusion, albeit a very persistent one."

Strange stuff. And what follows is an impossible task. In a few paragraphs — because this is all the time some of you may give me—I need to convince you that there are no discrete, solid objects out there. I'll explain in simple terms why—and don't you dare skip it! You do want to solve all your life's problems, don't you? Then there's something you must grasp clearly now. Soon you'll see the connection.

Matter is made of atoms bonded together. Familiar enough—we learned that in school. For example, the drinking glass on your kitchen counter is a complex molecular structure consisting primarily of silicon and oxygen atoms bonded together.

We would probably assume the mass of the glass is mostly the protons and neutrons, which make up 99 percent of the mass of every silicon and oxygen atom in the glass. And, back when electrons, protons, and neutrons were thought to be the smallest, most basic of particles, we'd have been right. Ah, the good old days!

Today, it's much more complicated. Now we know that protons and neutrons are themselves composed of even tinier particles—quarks. So, with this knowledge, we can conclude that the mass of the glass is the total mass of all the quarks.

And *here* is where it gets interesting. Quarks, compared to protons, are practically massless! Instead of mass (as we've conventionally understood it), we have interactions between massless particles and an energy field called the Higgs field, creating—you guessed it—*vibrations*.

These interactions slow down the particles' movement, which results in a condition we interpret as solid—the way we thought of the glass. This integral connection between energy and mass is reflected in Einstein's famous equation, $E = mc^2$, which reveals that mass itself is a form of energy.

We have been all wrong! What we have called matter is energy, whose vibration has been lowered as to be perceptible to the senses.

— Albert Einstein

Matter, as we know now, consists overwhelmingly, if not entirely, of emptiness. On hearing that, my friend Scott said: "That's not what the scale tells me!"

No matter how violently this notion may seem to contradict our senses, the universe is essentially a big *field* of energy. Energy can be described as oscillation. These oscillations are quantum physics phenomena. In more familiar language, they're waves, *vibrations*. Einstein wrote: "There is no place in this new kind of physics both for the field and matter, for the field is the only reality."

Reread the paragraph above three or four times, please, won't you? Repeat it to yourself throughout the day: ... *the field is the only reality*. In a way, this is the only affirmation we need. In the whole infinite universe, all that exists is "the field."

Solving our life's problems might be directly connected with the major unsolved problem in physics, known popularly as: The Theory of Everything. Physicists have been pursuing it actively since the early 1920s.

The Theory of Everything, the Grand Unified Theory, as it's technically called, will have to unite the four fundamental forces of the universe — electromagnetism, the strong and weak nuclear forces, and gravitation—in a single coherent system. Physicists' theories and models account for the first three of these forces. Their models work stunningly well—with great observational and experimental backup—for electromagnetism and the two nuclear forces. Not yet, however, for gravitation.

However, physicists are working on it. String theory is, so far, the strongest candidate in the cause. That work has led many theoretical physicists to the notion that at the root of every "particle" lie "strings"—incredibly tiny loops of energy. How tiny? Think in terms like billionth of a billionth of a billionth of a millimeter. All those loops oscillate, or vibrate.

Extremely simplified, the string theory comes down to this: These strings oscillate in different directions, different orientations, creating the appearance of what we familiarly call *particles* of varied sorts.

Because there is no hard evidence to support the existence of such strings, there's still much disagreement among physicists. So what? No crucial matter for us here, whether string theory or some other theory will eventually become that Theory of Everything, the fact remains: quantum physics shows that our everyday worldview is deeply flawed.

According to the new physics, there are no colors, no sounds, and no solid physical world "out there"—there are only electromagnetic waves. Our senses and our brains are partners in a complex feedback process, "creating" our perception of reality.

Once we orbited the Earth, we could no longer deny that it really is round. Likewise, to insist on our old notions of common sense physical reality is becoming less and less an intelligent option. Bottom line: We can't go much further in the old paradigm.

If you want to find the secrets of the Universe, think in terms of energy, frequency, and vibration.

— Nikola Tesla

If we want complete freedom from our problems, then we'll need to stop considering our senses as perfect experts on reality. Frontier science says they're anything but. Start thinking in terms of the always-charged energy field that surrounds us all. No, you don't need to worry about Higgs bosons and beta-particle decay, just embrace the metaphor of the energy field.

If you observe a person who's successful and fulfilled in life, you see a person who's been using the principles of quantum physics — knowingly or not. Instead of seeing a predictable world of solid obstacles and immovable barriers, the successful person sees a world that flows and vibrates, continually changing, alive with possibilities.

It's your worldview that defines your pool of possibilities. Bigger worldview… more options. You *can* shape your life any way you want! And you can start *now*!

CHAPTER 5

Quantum Superpowers...
Can We Tap Into Them?

B ack in 2004, our son Nikolai urged my husband and me to see an independent documentary film, *What the Bleep Do We Know?* — a film about a far-reaching implication of quantum physics. As some of you know, the film's core idea is that the material world is the product of individual and group consciousness.

My husband squirmed in his seat, glancing around sheepishly, lest someone from our church was there. This wasn't what we'd been hearing from the church pulpit. He wasn't ready to accept what was happening on screen. Neither was I.

At the same time, I found myself immensely intrigued. I knew after leaving the movie theatre that I'd be headed to the local bookstore to get all I could find on quantum physics and its mind-boggling implications.

Before coming to America, I used to teach physics to high school students and was already familiar with the basics of quantum mechanics. For example, I knew that light in some respects behaves as a wave, in others as a particle. The electrons and atoms we generally consider as being particles exhibit the properties of waves. Counterintuitive by itself, but there's more.

I remembered the double-slit experiment that is the cornerstone of quantum physics. Here's a greatly simplified version: If an electron is left unobserved, it exhibits wave properties, but the moment we want to measure its physical properties — mass, for example — the electron becomes a particle. It's the observer's *attention,* or its absence, that determines how the electron would behave — whether it remains a wave or becomes a particle.

The double-slit experiment, which has been performed in many variations since Thomas Young's original experiment in 1801, shook the foundations of classical physics. Everything super-small is neither wave nor particle. Rather, your focus, your observation, or lack thereof, will determine what properties it will exhibit. It does seem that when it comes to the subatomic level, it's as if we are the very creators of what happens.

The film was telling me I could influence more than electrons. By attuning my own thought patterns, I could influence even the unfolding of my life... Initially, it was hard to swallow. But after reading numerous books on the subject and chewing upon it thoroughly, it started to make more sense.

You've surely heard of the law of attraction. Its currently popular form is manifested in the 2006 film and book, *The Secret,* but the concept has been around for a long time. It's based on the 1890s popular philosophy of Judge Thomas Troward, a key figure in the "Science of Mind" movement of the time, though he doesn't use the term *law of attraction* explicitly.

You'll find the phrase used, though, in the 1906 *Thought Vibration or The Law of Attraction in the Thought World*. There, author William Walker Atkinson uses the term to explain roughly the version known today—the notion that "like attracts like," and in particular, that a positive mental attitude and focus can bring about what a person wants.

The notion has become well known, so to some it will seem old hat. But it's one thing to "know" something, quite another to live it. Unless you use a tool or concept consciously, day by day, you don't benefit from it.

Here is the reasoning and imagery I use to remind myself how the law of attraction *is* working, and to make it work on my terms.

The entire Universe, top to bottom, is comprised of energy. Things vibrate. And each thing has some particular characteristic frequency, which is called its *resonance frequency.*

Our brain activity is itself composed of electromagnetic waves or vibrations, as measured via the electroencephalograph (EEG). So, it stands to reason that our thoughts and feelings are also patterns of electromagnetic energy. Every emotion we have also has a resonance frequency, which can be changed.

For demonstrating the law of attraction, I find a radio analogy most helpful.

A radio uses an antenna to capture radio waves. It extracts only those waves with the desired frequencies. As those in the know put it, the radio separates *signal* from *noise*. The radio's amplifier increases the amplitude of incoming signals, making them stronger.

There's a tuner, too — a combination of an inductor and a capacitor, which form a circuit that resonates at a particular frequency, the *resonance frequency*. This type of circuit tends to block any signals at frequencies above or below the resonance frequency. You adjust that resonance frequency by turning the knob or pushing the button on your radio, (for example, FM-100), matching your favorite station's frequency.

Every possible station is present among the limitless vast range of frequencies. You just have to tune in. Likewise, everything you could possibly want already exists, as a quantum possibility. To see this possibility as part of your reality, you need to change the resonance frequency of the tuner — that's you — to match the frequency of the experience you want.

Now, once you've tuned in to your favorite station — say, the feeling of a fit, trim version of yourself — you'd best pay attention to what this station is broadcasting. Tune in, and suddenly you'll get a great discount membership offer at the best gym in town. Or someone invites you to a yoga class — at *just* the right time and place for you, or sends you a nice, new juicer as a birthday gift.

Although some people are tuning into the station: "The buffet is now open!" Be aware of what stations you're tuning into daily.

Definitely, there is more to it. For example, there are rules you need to obey to make a wish happen the way you want it, and we'll discuss them in the following chapters. But they can be learned and mastered easily with practice.

I know this idea of "creating reality" sounds looney at first. But it's only a hint of the future that's coming. Consider how the iPhone and iPad naturally and seamlessly have become putty in the hands of our children, while some of us who are older still don't know the difference between uploading and downloading. In the same way, this "creating reality" idea will be very easy for the next generation to grasp. However, *you* can start mastering it now.

A general knowledge of quantum phenomena, where physics encounters consciousness, is becoming as important as knowing the multiplication tables. The good news is that to understand quantum theory at a basic level, no math is needed. You can understand quantum theory's major implications with no knowledge of general physics, either. Whether you're five years old or a hundred and five, you can get it.

Watch some of the YouTube videos on the subject — for example: *Easy Quantum Mechanics*. In that video, the "mystery" presented by quantum physics appears right up front in a simple demonstration of the two-slit experiment.

With the development of a quantum computer, our old worldview will come crashing down. Our worldview shift won't be as gradual as accepting that the Earth is round. It's entirely possible that quantum theory will be taught in kindergarten, and that might be just a few years away. Move over, ABCs.

Watching that film, *What the Bleep Do We Know?* I imagined how people must have felt when they were told that the Earth wasn't flat, after all. We incur a similar shock when we realize our senses are deceiving us about the world around us.

What would you call a group of people who knew the world was round before this became common knowledge? You might back then have written them off as cultists, as heretics, as adherents of a bizarrely false religion. But it was none of that.

They simply possessed a truth not yet accepted by everyone else. Now, quantum mechanics is handing us powerful, fascinating implications, not yet generally accepted, offering new truths to anyone with an open mind.

CHAPTER 6

The Law of the Universe: Let It Be!

A classic American post-World War II film, *The Best Years of Our Lives,* centers on the story of Homer, a young sailor who comes home with a life-changing injury—the loss of his hands. Now equipped instead with hooks, he fears he's lost his girl, lost his chance of making a good livelihood, and lost his dream of playing the piano.

Does Homer, by the film's end, succeed in realizing all three of his dreams? I encourage you to watch the movie, if you haven't seen it yet.

I connect with Homer. Since suffering with my damaged hips since childhood, (from the earliest moment I can recall), I always wanted to dance. As a teen, I'd come home from school and pretend to be a dancer. In my condition, it took a lot of pretending.

The dream of dancing has carried on through my adult years, right up to the arrival of my fiftieth birthday and beyond. That dream is as tough as crabgrass. Whatever I do, it just won't go away.

For years now, I've been taking yoga classes, to get my legs and the rest of my body ready for dancing. Recently, we moved to California to be nearer my husband's family. Nick spearheaded the house search. I placed only one condition on his choice: the house had to be close to a yoga studio. Sure enough, we found the perfect combination.

Then, for two months, Nick and I had the same conversation—I kept telling him I was getting better and better in my yoga class and soon would be able to start my belly dancing classes. Nick's exasperated response was, "You're kidding me, right?!" He's rather conservative, religiously, so he didn't like this idea one bit.

Upon leaving my yoga class one day, I decided: *Today* I'm going to look for a belly dancing studio. That afternoon, when pulling into our driveway, I knew something was amiss. Nick stood there, outside, arms crossed. His face didn't look like he'd just won the lottery. My best guess: a plumbing problem.

"You're not gonna believe this," he calls out. "I'm in the house eating breakfast and, all of a sudden, I get this urge to meet the neighbors. You know—across the back fence. So I go to their front door..." By now Nick was rolling his eyes. "You won't believe what they've got going on over there!"

My imagination swirled, and I thought of all the unpleasant curiosities a couple might find among the neighbors.

"A beer joint?" I ventured.

"Almost," he said, shaking his head. He looked me in the eye and said, stressing every syllable: "A be-lly dan-cing studio!"

"Oh, my world!" I exclaimed. "Don't you see? God

wants me to dance!"

Our neighbor was indeed a belly dancing instructor. I could see the studio from our bedroom window. Things just couldn't get any better.

Educated as I was as a mathematician, I knew the probability of such an outcome occurring randomly was approaching zero. But if it wasn't chance or coincidence, what was it? Could it be that my desire to dance was so great that my thoughts *created* what I wished for?

Can science prove the law of attraction? Asking that is like asking whether science can prove the existence of God. No physicist could offer such a "proof" without risking his reputation. That doesn't mean, however, that science can't offer some encouragement from the sidelines.

Here's one bold implication that I favor. The quantum field that surrounds us has the potential to become *anything* in response to the energy you animate by thinking particular thoughts and feeling particular feelings. It's your observation, your participation, and even more, your expectations that command the quantum field to manifest into concrete, distinct, material things.

Physicists dash off all manner of zippy phrases to describe this sort of thing: "collapsing the quantum possibility wave." You, on the other hand, only need to get a robust grip on the notion that your *attention* creates the world in which you live.

My belly dancing episode was an *Aha!* moment, when I realized I *could* bring whatever I'm passionate about into my life. It even affected my no-nonsense, oh-so-practical husband.

Not even once did he object to my dancing since that day.

I like the following anecdote to remind me to watch my thoughts. I first heard it in Russian. Here's my best translation...

One day, an angel decided he'd help someone fulfill a dream. Descending from heaven, he stepped onto a bus, picking out the first person he saw — a woman on her way to work. The angel decided to read her thoughts and learn her most cherished dream: *Whatever's most prominent in her thoughts — that's what I'll give her.*

Life is so dreadful, the woman thought. *Dreary... painful... and unfair. It's endless crap, crap, crap.* And the woman's mental lament continued for the whole bus ride.

Ahhh, thought the angel. Now he knew what the woman wanted and decreed: *Let it be!* He left thinking: *Hmm...Crap... Why would she need so much of it?*

Despite its crudeness, the angel story offers a good illustration of how the law of attraction operates. The vibe you *give* is the vibe you'll *get.*

We've all had thoughts along the lines of the woman on the bus. Down in the dumps over a lousy job, a layoff, aches and pains, a difficult relationship, money worries or loneliness. Some of us have indulged those thoughts obsessively, making them part of our persona, our self-image. *I'm ugly... I can't ever find romance... I'll never find a good job...* Most of us, at some time, have lived inside our negative thoughts and accordingly made them self-fulfilling prophecies.

Do you see now how you need to take *full* responsibility for the life you're experiencing? You can be creating it consciously. Or you're creating it by default — by simply "letting things happen" and ignoring, even ruling out, the possible solutions to your problems.

We all live under universal laws. Just as we observe the laws of gravity and electricity, we must respect other laws that govern our life. One day, science will have a good, sound, comprehensive theory on the law of attraction. Meanwhile, what we care about is that the law *works*, and we can use it to improve our lives.

Even before Newton formulated the law of gravity, people knew better than to violate it, like *never drop an anvil on your toe*. The same is true with the law of attraction. Once you're aware of it, you'll see how it manifests itself in *your* life, and in everyone else's life as well.

My desire to defeat my disability, in the most daring fashion, was more than a passing fancy. It wasn't a mere abstraction. It was palpable. And it materialized: despite my very busy schedule, I've been granted the opportunity to dance almost every day.

Whether or not science has "proved" it, your destiny can be yours to control. And that, I love!

A person is what he or she thinks about all day long.

— Ralph Waldo Emerson

Our guardian angel, or God, or Universal Love (whatever you choose to call the master of your universe), *will* give you everything you want. This Higher Power doesn't share our perception of good or bad—it knows only love. Operating according to universal laws, it sends you what you're vibrating. Things within the field of possibility will match the vibration frequencies of the energy you emanate. In other words, they will resonate with your feelings and thoughts and become manifested in your life.

See the world through this lens, and you'll become better at recognizing the law of attraction working in *your* daily life. Whatever you want in life, be sure it is ever-present in your thoughts. Live it, breathe it. Keep it as close to you as your heartbeat. And remember: angels are floating around, tuning into what is going on in your head. And all they ever decree is "Let it be!"

Dreary... painful... and unfair life. "Let it be!" *Playing the piano.* "Let it be!" *Dancing.* "Let it be!" What are *you* thinking as you're riding the bus of your life?

CHAPTER 7

Blessings... Nothing but Blessings

B*less you! God's blessings! May the Lord bless you!* We hear these kinds of wishes often, and heartfelt they are. And what do we consider a "blessing" to be?

I used to wonder about my plight — multiple surgeries, years of pain, some real misery in childhood, being and feeling so different from the other kids, so isolated... Who would ever wish such experiences on a loved one? Definitely, in the eyes of the world, these are *not* blessings. Still, I wouldn't change a thing. I would never have achieved what I now cherish, had I not experienced those "blessings."

Want to solve your problems? It's time to change your attitude toward them.

Socrates said: *If all our misfortunes were laid in one common heap whence everyone must take an equal portion, most people would be content to take their own and depart.* In modern parlance: *If we all threw our problems in a pile and saw everyone else's, we'd just grab our own back and get lost.*

Why? We can lament their unfairness, bemoan their heaviness and harshness, but they're *ours*.

We *esteem* our problems… we *perpetuate* our problems… and in some peculiar way, we *need* our problems. We even deserve our problems. No, I don't mean we deserve the "punishment." I mean we deserve the *opportunities they offer us* to learn. Problems arise to help us strive for new solutions, experiment with new ways, and to change our lifestyles for the better.

Imagine a woman who wants to shed unwanted pounds and improve her overall health. She sticks to those goals with determination, yearning fervently to be slimmer, fitter. Yet, she doesn't like healthful foods and can't find the will to exercise. She wants good health and is unhappy with her current level of fitness, but does nothing to change the status quo.

This goes on for weeks, months, even years, until finally some crisis forces her into action — a trip to the emergency room, a breakup with a boyfriend, or the prospect of surgery, as was my case. She can no longer afford to resist and finds ways to accomplish her goals. She implements new lifestyle changes, plucks up the courage to exercise, and finds the will to eat healthy.

Problems bring change. They force us to act, and act fast. We need problems to instigate development, to give us a push in the right direction, and to help us avoid stagnation.

As with our woman, forces of desire and resistance can create an endless counterbalance. The arrival of a problem often becomes that third force, compelling us to change, to grow physically, emotionally, and spiritually.

Seeing the negative can help us see what's positive. Consider… we generally don't feel health. We only feel the *absence* of health. Once we've known sickness, we can appreciate health. Without negative experiences, we couldn't appreciate the positive. Without sadness, how could we know happiness? We need contrast. You can't see white on white. Or black on black. But, white on black, its opposite, is vivid.

In the world we live, negativity is a part of life. Trying to get rid of it completely is futile, foolish, and impossible.

I laughed so hard I cried. Life abounds with that positive-negative duality. Even if handed to us, we couldn't tolerate too much positivity — not without turning it into some negativity. If we don't have problems, we'll create them. To have everything with nothing to strive for is a precariously unstable state, and can lead a person to that pattern of behavior we call "looking for trouble."

My future husband, when I met him, was 17. I was 18. We were attending the same university. He was big, strong, and good-looking. So many things had come easy to Nick — sports, games, becoming popular among fellow students. He even had that annoying ability to get a passing grade in any given subject without ever cracking the books.

It was all *too* easy. Without a care in the world, he'd slid into bad company, drinking, fights, and reckless motorcycle driving. Then he met me — a girl who would hold his hand, even for walking. Nick had so much to give, and finally he'd found someone who could use a lot of help.

People said I'd made a good catch, that I'd somehow reeled him in like a fish. But it was the other way around. I never encouraged that kind of connection, knowing well that we were so very different. But Nick clung to me as if I were his life pre-server. *We've nothing in common,* I said many times. But it didn't shake him off.

Looking back, it seems he *needed* to take upon himself some of my problems and my life's challenges to ground him, to give him purpose, to take him away from his self-destructive behavior.

I'm convinced: If we don't have a problem, we'll go find one. We need problems for our growth and development.

Some problems dwell with us for a week, others for months, and some "torment" us for years. Yet, the lifelong negative issues, conditions and situations we view as problems hold the potential to help us remake our lives.

Take my nephew, Chris. When Chris was only nine months old, his father divorced his mother, and afterward surfaced only sporadically in his son's life. Chris longed for his father's attention, reaching out to him many times through his teens and young adult years. His father never participated in his son's life — he didn't even come to his wedding.

Chris suffered that rejection intensely, as he had always sought his father's recognition. Chris strove to become an architect, like his father, and he succeeded. Now he's traveling worldwide, working for a prominent architectural firm, building the most spectacular houses. Finally, he did get his father's approval, but there's even more. In seeking to resolve his childhood trauma, he found his true calling.

Great personal victories can often have their roots in big life-defying problems.

Sigmund Freud developed his theory of psychoanalysis during the period in which he experienced severe depression and nightmares. His condition prompted a "self-analysis" of his own dreams and childhood memories.

Winston Churchill became the finest orator in Parliament, despite his stuttering. He went to great lengths to learn not to stutter, rehearsing and rewriting his speeches endless times, memorizing each one thoroughly. As a result, he's considered one the most outstanding public speakers of the twentieth century.

The world knows Bruce Willis as an A-list actor, but few know that he, too, struggled with stuttering through his first twenty years. Willis never did achieve Churchill's fluency, but he found victory another way. He used his stuttering as the springboard for humor, learning to stand out as the joker in the crowd. "A big part of my sense of humor came out of my stuttering," Willis observed. "In trying to overcome that and have some dignity, I said, 'Yes, I stutter, but I can make you laugh.'"

People often tell me that they couldn't "find themselves." Here's how I see it... Your existing strengths, of course, are important in choosing your calling in life, but if you're using only your strengths, and have to hide your weaknesses, you are in the wrong business! Find ways you can use those faults and drawbacks to your advantage.

Often, our persisting problems point us to what we should be doing. Example: A parent whose child has Down syndrome started a non-profit organization to help families affected by this condition. Two guys in Hawaii, both with celiac disease (which prevents them from eating foods containing gluten) started a restaurant—now a chain—specializing in 100% gluten-free food. Or a person with huge feet—never able to find the right size in shoe stores—started a successful Internet business selling large-size shoes.

To all these folks, their jobs were custom-made just for them. These reflective individuals recognized the power hidden within their problems, and saw how every problem contains the seeds of its own solution.

In my work, I've met dozens of people whose major health issues were resolved by eating entirely or mostly raw vegan foods. Afterward, they wrote books, conducted seminars, and became healthy-lifestyle promoters.

One acquaintance, Elaine, for four years strove to heal her breast cancer — the natural way — and was successful. Now, she's considering leaving her nursing job to start her own business as a colon hydrotherapist.

Be attentive to the problems that have troubled you all through your life! Overcoming your apparent non-blessings has the potential to change your life profoundly and lead you toward finding your own path in life, your vocation, and your destiny.

When reflecting on my problems, I clearly see they were simply signposts to direct me to my calling. At age thirteen, my classmate — quite physically beautiful she was — told me that she "couldn't imagine living" if she looked like me, plain and limping. I'm sure she didn't mean to hurt me. It was just one of those thoughts people spit out, without considering its effect.

The distress I experienced in childhood prompted me to passionately search for the secrets of physical beauty. That, in turn, led me to finding and embracing some of the key anti-aging practices in my forties. Now, in my fifties, I'm often complimented on my youthful looks, and life is *so* much more fun today than when I was a teenager. What's more, I've made a career out of helping others improve their health and appearance.

Every problem we consider negative in our lives is there for a reason: to create desire for its opposite. The very purpose of problems occurring in our lives is to realize what we *don't* want, and by negating that, we'll discover what we *do* want from life.

Stop focusing on what you don't want and on the cloud of doom that surrounds it. Stop giving it energy, or you'll be attracting more of the same. Instead, focus on the opposite, that the "negative" was put there to facilitate.

If life held no challenges, we'd never accomplish anything. Nor would it occur to us that there might *be* something wonderful to strive for. We need problems. We need the struggle of overcoming them in order to evolve, and become our best.

It can be outright wonderful, I say, to have a problem. I'm grateful for my life's trials. They have made me who I am now.

Once you appreciate your problem fully, you can dig to its root, to a lack that you feel, and begin to make changes.

CHAPTER 8

In Your Face

When I was thirteen my parents took me to Bulgaria, to a beautiful beach resort. We'd been living in a closed, austere Soviet Union, and this was our first visit abroad. On the beach, a tall, graying gentleman stepped up to my mom and asked her in broken Russian what was wrong with my legs. Mom volunteered some information about my condition, despite my disapproving stare.

He offered that he was an American orthopedic surgeon, working with a new hip joint technology that he felt sure would help me. On a scrap of paper, he wrote his address and phone number and told my mom to send him my x-rays at her earliest convenience. He intimated he'd do all he could to bring me to the USA for treatment.

My mom got hopeful. I got fearful. All I saw in this kind offer was the prospect of more surgeries. I already had seven and was determined not to let doctors "hurt me" any more. I nagged my mom to destroy the doctor's note, and I wouldn't let up until she grew weary of my bulldogging and tore it up.

That summer was the last I could enjoy the beach as only a child could, without regard to my skewed body. Two months later, back in school, everything changed. I grew up. I *had* to be pretty—it's the law of teenage life for girls everywhere. I became ready to endure *anything* to make myself "normal."

But there was nothing in the Soviet Union that could help me. Yet the solution had already been handed to me—literally, on that scrap of paper—even before I'd fully grasped the problem that would become the prevailing one in my life for years to come.

I came to the USA twenty years later and had those hip replacement surgeries. How much different those twenty years might have been for me, had I not been so shortsighted and compelled my mother to tear up that doctor's note. Apparently, I had some lessons to learn. Here's a good one: Life isn't meant to be so hard—we *make* it so, by resisting.

This world in which we live, the material world, is polarized. Positive and negative are equally present. Always. They are integral parts of life. No problem exists, then, without a solution. And it's *always* right there in front of us. This is true whether or not we see the solution, whether or not we even acknowledge that there is a problem.

Let me illustrate this with another story… Just after my first hip surgery, the prospect was: I'd be recovering alone, at home. I knew I had to cleanse my system after my surgeries. My husband's job took him away from home a week at a time. So the question was: How would I go about making those daily juices and other raw food dishes, gimping about on crutches?

I needed help. And sure enough, it appeared in the form of a charming woman, Susan, a breast cancer survivor. She thought of herself as being entirely cured and was determined to enjoy life. Susan offered to help me, and I accepted gratefully. For three months she came daily and prepared fresh green juices for the mornings and salads for later.

I always invited her to join me in juicing, reasoning that if I needed cleansing after surgery, so did she. She always declined politely. "Not my cup of tea," she said.

Five years and two weeks after she'd been pronounced cancer-free, Susan's cancer came back with a vengeance. Thanks to my interest in natural healing, I've become acquainted with numerous people whose cancers have gone into remission or disappeared entirely on an all-raw vegan lifestyle that included daily green juices.

In fact, as I'm writing this, a powerful documentary, *The Truth About Cancer: A Global Quest,* has been just released. It's exactly the sort of explosive material — "too controversial" for major media — that I encourage you to explore.

It's about how people are going against mainstream medical approaches to cancer. They've beaten cancer, and moreover, have become much healthier in the result. I so wish Susan had been one of them…

Solutions, answers, and remedies stare us in the face, and we don't even know it.

This morning's yoga class provided yet another example. Karen, the studio's owner, was telling us about her family reunion. Her uncle was always complaining about back pain. Every once in a while he'd bend forward, trying to relieve his discomfort. Karen, a compassionate person, saw yoga as an answer, and started telling her uncle about it.

What was the man's reaction? The usual: No…it's not for me… I'm just not flexible enough. Karen insisted, and told her uncle she'd seen many people in worse shape try yoga, and they found it immensely helpful.

She also told him that back bends would be very healing for someone in his condition—an idea contrary to what most people would presume. And he should do *back* bends rather than forward ones. At this point Karen's uncle got nasty: *What do you know? If you'd spent thirty years in construction like me, you wouldn't be doing silly postures now.*

I don't know whether or not the man eventually took his niece's advice, but my point remains the same. Where there is a *problem*, there is a *solution*. The key: Just look. The solution is usually staring you in the eyes.

Why don't we recognize solutions when they're presented to us? One possible reason: The solution often appears at the same time the problem does, or even before we quite realize we even have a problem. Thus, we're not quite ready to see it, sometimes we're unmotivated to see it.

Examine your life carefully, and I'll wager that you too will see occasions when you were virtually handed the solution to a problem, but simply didn't see it.

What will make the solution appear? It's your belief that this solution exists and your keen attention to life around you.

Problems always come disguised as lessons we need to learn. And we learn the most not from those who hold similar views, but from those with whom we disagree.

Consider these cases—an American doctor who offered me his help… my offer to Susan to add green juices to her diet…or Karen's advice to her uncle to try yoga for his back pain. In each case, a solution was offered from a point of view, which was totally disagreeable to the recipient. Remember: each time a disagreeable idea is thrust in your face, *pay attention to it.*

Begin facing life with a *Yes* attitude. Start by seeing what's coming your way. Pay attention to that new person you meet today. Pay attention to the title of the book or article recommended to you, or to the unsolicited advice of an old friend, excited about some new experience.

These are signposts for you to follow, as is this book. You're reading it for a reason. Maybe today's the day your paradigm shifts, and your new life begins!

Quantum physics teaches that we are not only the *observers* of reality but also the *participants*. These days, if I come across an idea I oppose, I acknowledge the fact: although someone else expressed it, ultimately it was *me* who created it, in response to *my* needs. It's another point of view I need to learn because it's presented to me for *my* growth. I am, after all, the center of my universe, as you are of yours. From my point of view, it's all about me. As for you, it's all about you.

See and receive it all. I urge you. Receive what light comes your way from every star and galaxy. From every person you encounter, every book you read, every film you watch, every theory or method or viewpoint you're privileged to face. There's something in there for *you.*

CHAPTER 9

The Games Your Mind Plays

Here's an old story, nonetheless still a stunning one. Professor John Wilson of the University of London described an incident he experienced in a remote area of Africa. He showed a film to teach sanitation methods to the local villagers—the first film any of them had ever seen. To Wilson's amazement, not one of the dozens of villagers watching the film could really see and grasp it. None saw the images *as* images.

Similarly, Aboriginal Australian villagers in the 1920s couldn't make any sense of photographs taken of them in their first encounter with photography. Both groups of villagers were unmotivated and unprepared to deal with the fruits of modern technology.

Both incidents illustrate a scientifically proven idea: We only experience what we believe possible. What we do not believe possible, we cannot fully experience.

I met my big embarrassment soon after arriving in the USA in 1991. I'm flustered to even write about it, but I believe it will illustrate my point nicely. In the Soviet Union, where I'd lived for my first 33 years, we had to open bottles, cans, or jugs, with a knife, a can opener, the edge of a table or window ledge, sometimes even with our teeth. And we definitely had to apply some force in doing so.

A nice American family from church invited us to dinner. As the lady of the house was setting the table, I offered to help. Our hostess — a sweet older lady — asked me to open a gallon jug of orange juice. Without thinking, I, who hold a degree in mechanical engineering with honors, took a knife and cut the top off the lid, quite ignoring the little tab I was supposed to pull. Now imagine the expression on my hostess' face. When the mistake became obvious to me, I learned the full meaning of the saying: *I wish the ground would open up and swallow me.*

Coming from the Soviet Union, not only had I never seen such a large container of orange juice before, but I never would have suspected opening it could be so easy. Gadgets and refinements simplifying everyday life had never been part of my experience, so I didn't *look* for something as simple as a tab to pull. Thus, I never saw it.

That's exactly how it is with life's problems. We never look at where the solution is, though it's right in front of us.

The computer gives a perfect analogy of how our brain works. When you begin typing something in your browser search bar, the computer tries to "help" you with each new character you type, offering you words from your previous searches, or from websites you've visited.

For example, though you intend to type in "Manitoba," the computer offers you a host of other words along the way, from "many" to "manifold." Just as you must forge on until you've typed in every letter you had intended, so you must resist your brain's "old" associations — your prior beliefs — getting in the way.

Cache. It used to mean only a hidden place, usually in the ground, to stash food, drink, and supplies. In today's computer terms, cache also refers to a place where data is stored for later retrieval and use. Research increasingly reveals that our brain works like a quantum computer — a *big* one.

Caching saves time and effort, avoiding overwork. The more information that can be supplied by a cache, as distinct from a brand new search, the more efficient our mental computer becomes. Think of yourself driving a car now, compared to when you were first learning how to drive.

When we receive new data via seeing, hearing, touching, tasting or smelling, our brain catalogs it and caches it. Presented with similar input, the brain goes directly to its cache to check for a match. It looks for *similarity* — not necessarily the one-to-one perfect match — and more often than not, finds it. This is how we assign phenomena, the objects of our perception, to categories — *Oh, yes, it's one of those...*

We've all seen, for example, a doppelganger — the stranger who looks so much like our friend Bill — that we greet him as such at the supermarket. Our brains play these tricks on us over and over, showing us patterns that aren't *quite* right. We'll eventually figure out that the new "Bill" isn't really our old Bill. Often, though, we don't figure out such things — ever. We buy into those mind-tricks without consciously recognizing them.

We all have a unique cache, built from the sum of our life

experiences. That's why each of us interprets the same information differently. In a sense, then, we don't see how things *are*, but rather how they *were*. Our past visions and categories shape our perceptions.

No one sees *truly* objectively, ever. We look at the world moment by moment, seeing it not exactly as it is, but constructing it instead from images past cached. So, we see it as we *are*.

We see the world *through* the lenses of our mind. It's the *lens* that makes a subject pretty or ugly, desirable or not. Pretty and ugly aren't *out there* — they're *in here*, in our mind.

Our past — our cache — always shapes our beliefs, and for some people, it does it quite rigidly. Doubt the world! Doubt a teacher, a writer, but *first* doubt your own mind!

How *do* we change our views? Two essential ingredients are required. One: new data. Two: a willingness to question — a skeptical spirit. That questioning needs to be directed not only outward, but also inward. Question mainly what is most sacred to you — the judgments, theories, and categories you find most fundamental.

Question the "obviously" true. Our *obvious* judgments and perceptions are mostly based on our cached data and memories. And they are the ones that are predominantly involved in our own mental self-trickery. Everything that is *obvious* to you may be very outdated.

When scientists studied the brain functions, they learned that consciousness finds what it wants to find. The human mind does not perceive what is "there," but what it *believes* should be there.

Our subconscious cache is a kind of place where we store

stories. And most of them are negative. We treasure what hurts. These stories prescribe and they circumscribe. They tell us what's "wrong with" us, what we can't do, what we shouldn't do, what we can never be. Those stories continue to play in our internal movie-house, our minds.

You know those old movies, you see and hear them in snippets all the time. Mrs. Lambert tells you with *those* math scores, you'll *never* get to be an engineer. Jed says *I think we should see other people* ... and you cry inside because this is not the first time. Other voices, some with no names: *It's your sister, the pretty one... You'll never fully recover from an injury like that...*

These thoughts have been programmed into us and have become much of who we are, of what we perceive as "self." But that's not to say we cannot change. The subconscious takes cues from our environment, it reacts to positivity and negativity as much as anything else in this world, and it can be changed and reprogrammed based on those reactions.

If you live a negative, bland, and lifeless existence, one of monotony, drained of all fun, your subconscious mind will become stale, stagnant, and uninspiring. It will continue to lead you down the path that you have taken until that point, ensuring that your life remains as dull, uninteresting, and boring as it has always been.

If, on the other hand, you inject some positivity into your existence, if you change your scenery, and if you show your subconscious mind that's *not* who you are, it will adapt.

We all know how marvelous it is to have a flexible and pliable body. It gives us comfort, smoothness, lightness, and ease in our movement. It's even more important to have that fluidity in your mind. Mental flexibility brings that lightness and joy to life itself.

In the wake of my orange juice tab embarrassment, I had to revise completely my old home-country ways and process new information, new experiences. When faced with life's challenges, we need to do the same.

CHAPTER 10

Pain... The Greatest Gift God Gives Us

You turn onto the Interstate, and as you're driving up the ramp, somewhat distracted by the conversation with your passenger — YIKES! You're going the wrong way — the wrong side of the road. Most of the signs are facing in the opposite direction, but thankfully, you do catch the one red sign that says WRONG WAY.

That's what pain is — a warning sign, telling you that your life is going in the wrong direction. What happens when you see that Interstate sign? If you're fortunate, you'll find a turnoff before a collision happens. That's your chance to correct your mistake before disaster strikes.

Physical pain is a warning, both necessary and natural. Pain tells the mind that something's not right, that our ways are wrong for joyful pain-free living, that we need to change our ways: to *do something* — something *different*, at least to stop causing more pain.

What do most us do instead? Pop a pill... the pain is

gone! And we continue doing the very same things over and over that cause the pain in the first place.

That darned CHECK ENGINE light again! You know it doesn't mean much—that's what your brother-in-law told you. So you ignore it. *Probably just some emissions thing.* It starts to bug you. So you have that same ever-wise brother-in-law disable it for you—just the snip of a wire and that annoying light is gone.

You keep driving. After all, the car's still working—right? Then... it goes dead. Your engine's thrown a rod.

Clearly, ignoring that little light was foolish. Taking medicines is a lot like ignoring that bothersome light. Yes, in a critical case you might need that antibiotic right now to fight an infection. But consider those "little pills"—curious how we trivialize them, isn't it?—that you take for blood pressure, high cholesterol, aches, and the like. Most of them are band-aids, not cures.

If all we do is deaden pain or "correct" numbers with pills, we're ignoring and masking the cause, and we're not addressing the *real* underlying issues. The aches, pains, and other symptoms that medical science calls disease are really indications of the body's heroic inner nature. It's always striving to correct itself, which is the natural process we need to take advantage of—not endless pills—if we want real health and wellness.

Here's an interesting thought: *Disease is the utmost expression of ignorance.* In other words: Getting a disease is an indication that you desperately need to learn something and staying sick is irrefutable evidence of your refusal to do so.

Your pain is the breaking of the shell that encloses your understanding.

— Khalil Gibran

On the road or off, for each of us there are life's lessons we need to learn. One way or another, we *will* learn them.

I endured much pain in my childhood and young adult years. Yet, I'm overwhelmingly grateful for the life I had, pain notwithstanding. Everything of value I've learned has come from pain. But my gratitude is for *past* pain. Like most of you, I want to avoid future pain.

Here is the lesson to remember. Moreover, if you take but one message from this book, let it be this... No matter what physical problem you may have, be it a damaged limb, diabetes, cancer, or what-have-you, there *is* a solution. It exists right *now*, and it's within your reach.

You'll need to alter what you're doing now, make changes to your lifestyle, and experiment with new ideas and different approaches to your problem. Looking for a solution to your physical challenge, you'll willingly open your mind for change. In other words, you'll choose to make changes, so improvements can occur.

On another note: most likely, you've already been exposed to the solution to your problem, somewhere, somehow, but have dismissed it. So what if you continue to ignore it? If you *don't* make any radical changes in your belief system, waiting for others to solve your problem, you'll still learn a lot, that's for sure. And you'll learn much of that from *pain*. Like your car, you might even throw a rod.

Do it… or don't do it. Either way, change is in store. Either way, you'll become a different person.

No matter what you've heard to the contrary, suffering is *not* a virtue. The only virtuous goal is to *end* suffering.

The pain, *per se*, is not suffering. What is suffering? It is a face-to-face encounter with something that part of us doesn't want to face. Suffering is the consequence of our *desire* for the pain to cease. You feel bad in response to the pain because you want to be free of it.

Don't wish for different circumstances. Rather, make your utmost effort to benefit from the situation you are in now. Dealing with the immediate pain can be a great transformative experience.

Acknowledge your pain. Recognize it rather than deny it. And don't "fight it." (You'll lose that one, anyway.) And don't escape it, especially not in a hazed, drug-induced state.

Pain is a messenger. See it! Hear it! Meet it and greet it! And thereby, release it!

Once you've acknowledged your pain, acknowledge what it is, (a natural healing response), as well as what it isn't, (a nasty "intruding influence" that can control you absolutely), then you've begun to win, and all without fighting.

Science confirms that we can control pain mentally — without the aid of drugs. (That is not what a pharmacist will tell you.) There's a structure in your brain that sets your threshold for pain. It's called the periaqueductal gray, or PAG. Your PAG is abundant in endorphins, opiate receptors, and many other beneficial substances powerfully related to information and emotion.

Whenever you hurt, your perception, your "decision" of whether it hurts a little, moderately, or agonizingly, passes through the PAG. It's your emotional state that determines how much pain you'll feel.

We're all familiar with that phenomenon. If you stub your toe while already feeling down, or perhaps annoyed, that toe's going to hurt something fierce, and may keep on that way. But stub that same toe the same way in the midst of a happy occasion, or perhaps in the middle of a life-threatening crisis, and it will hurt much less.

How does it all work? Neurons in your frontal cortex project down into your PAG, giving you a degree of *conscious* control over the degree of pain or alertness you experience.

Bottom line: You can, to a greater or lesser degree, *choose* how to interpret the stimuli around you, and pain stimuli in particular. It's your call as to how much it hurts.

Do not think of an injury or a disease as something hateful or something to escape. Learn from it! Ask the question: What is the purpose of me experiencing this pain or illness? We must study any given disease or injury just as carefully as any other condition we wish to correct.

Pain is your adviser. Pain is your guide, informing you that you've strayed away from your true being and the laws of nature. It implores you to make changes to find the correct path, to stay true to yourself, and create the life that is meant for you.

Much of your pain is the bitter potion by which the physician within you heals your sick self.

— Kahlil Gibran

We can avoid all manner of difficulties and problems, and save ourselves a ton of grief, *if* we'd open ourselves up to the possibilities of life and go along willingly, without rushing headlong into inherent danger. The choice is yours!

CHAPTER 11

A Shortcut to a Better Life

The first sixteen years of my marriage were unhappy. Ironically, it was because my husband Nick had a strong desire to make me happy... *his* way. With the attitude "husband knows best," Nick wanted to rule the family as master of his domain. But subservience wasn't in my nature. We disagreed on *everything*. I felt emotionally drained and harbored growing resentment.

At the lowest point of my marriage I finally grasped it: I *can't change my husband*. How could I? I couldn't even make him listen to me for more than ten seconds without his retorting, "It's all in your head." (It's only now, writing this book, that I realize how right, in a way, he was!) I had to do *something*, change *something*. I knew I needed to be proactive, or I would just lose it.

It was at that time that I came across a book by Paul Bragg—*The Miracle of Fasting*. Inspired by this book, I started to fast regularly, every Friday, for 24 to 36 hours. All the spaghetti and meatballs, pizza, sloppy joes, hot dogs, frozen dinners, even my precious morning cappuccinos, all disappeared from my diet. I lost at least 30 pounds. My health and appearance improved dramatically. My disposition improved, too. And, miraculously, my marriage started to get better.

But why? Problems — interpersonal ones, especially — are often matters of perception. You're the observer. If *you* change, your *observations* will change.

So you have problems: relationships, job, and money, all increasingly pressing. For you to feel better, you think, circumstances need to change. Others need to change. But what are your chances?

A truthful, more honest view: *You're* the problem. Start there. You're living in your body, so start your cleanup right at home. One of the surest ways to improve your life is to upgrade your diet. It doesn't matter where you are right now — you can start from anywhere. How would an upgrade in your diet look?

Transitioning to a vegetarian diet is, all by itself, capable of changing your life profoundly, though a bit oddly. When you stop eating boxed cereals, nobody notices. When you stop eating cookies, nobody pays any attention. But the moment you say "no" to a slice of Thanksgiving turkey and declare, *Oh, I'm vegetarian now*, people get nervous. You're… hmmm… "different." One of *those* people… Interestingly, alcoholics who quit drinking get the same reaction. They are, to their friends, no longer "normal."

A further example of a diet upgrade, beyond vegetarian, is going vegan. This means you stop eating *all* animal products, including eggs, dairy and fish.

Still, a diet upgrade isn't necessarily about conversion to

some particular dietary philosophy. There are, in truth, quite a few diet variations out there that are quite good. But no matter what diet you choose, let it, please, include two things. First, eliminate processed foods. Second, add more natural, wholesome foods—the more raw vegan food items, the better—to your meals.

You may remember in the 1980s when doctors first told us that eating processed food carries health hazards, that we were to eat five servings of fruits and vegetables every day, and cut down on processed foods. And this is a good start.

At age 37, I saw how processed food was making me overweight and unhealthy. I took this basic advice further, decided to cut out *all* processed foods and started making my meals from raw fruits and vegetables, raw nuts and seeds. (Yes, you can do it! Just visit my website **www.beautifulonraw.com** for a big selection of delicious raw food recipes.)

Two years after going vegetarian, I moved gradually to a raw vegan lifestyle. My life hasn't been the same since. Sure, there was an initial cleansing involved, a couple of rough spots on the way, but it was all worth it. I became healthier, full of youthful energy, and my overall looks improved enough to draw constant complements.

What's so special about raw plant foods? We've learned a lot about carbohydrates, proteins, lipids, vitamins, etc. All of these are "things," separate *parts*. This type of thinking blocks our seeing the profound interconnectedness of all that exists. Ultimately, there are no "parts" at all in this vast web. Living plants aren't just "sources" of this protein or that mineral. Instead, it's a terrain of intermingling energies, where everything influences everything else.

Medical and nutritional sciences still operate in Newtonian physics. If you're in med school or doing a master's in nutritional science, you're not required to study quantum mechanics.

We're taught to think of the atom in terms of little balls rotating about one another. That's handy. Familiar. And wrong. There are no billiard balls at all inside the atom. No "things." Go way down to the subatomic level, and you'd see—if you could "see" this at all—a network of relations, of energies.

Recent research shows that our cells' nuclei function as bio-computers, moving information at what we once thought was an "impossible" speed. Biophysicist and molecular biologist Peter Garyaev and his colleagues have proved, both theoretically and experientially, their hypothesis that cells do indeed exchange information instantaneously.

The term *entanglement* is a key concept in understanding this instant cell communication. On the quantum level, any two objects that interact become entangled. After that, what happens to one object instantaneously influences the other—no matter how far apart they are.

Garyaev based his research on a phenomenon predicted by Einstein, Podolsky, and Rozen in 1935. They suggested that when two entangled photons move apart from one another, and one of them collides with another object, that colliding photon would disappear, and the information it carried would be instantaneously transferred to the other photon. Thus, one photon would "turn into" another. This quantum phenomenon later became known as "teleportation."

Austrian scientists proved in 1997 that a photon can be

teleported — instantly moved from one place to another — with all the information intact. Our DNA, it's suggested, works this same way. We have innumerable metabolic processes going on in trillions of living cells, and each one of those cells constantly "knows" everything about all the others, thanks to "entangled" photons.

This idea offers a new level of understanding of biology and genes, as well as of live organisms and plants. And yes, it puts a different spin on nutrition and food preparation.

Unless we begin to view our food items from a quantum perspective, we'll never fully realize the superiority of raw unprocessed foods. We'll keep hearing that cooked food is just as good or even better than raw, based on its chemical composition alone.

Living plant foods, down to the last particle of their atomic structure, are highly organized, intricately beautiful, and "intelligent." The way I see it: cooking and any other kind of processing compromises the food's integrity, making it less "intelligent," less able to offer you strength and health. Hopefully, these are the main reasons you eat them in the first place.

Living food — with no or as little processing as possible — is the only food that can "communicate" with your body, assuring your long, healthy life. Read my earlier books, such as *Quantum Eating*, and you'll be convinced.

Start simple. Just include more and more raw vegan foods in your diet, increasing their percentage as your body adjusts. Here's what happens every time we upgrade our diet: We experience cleansing on emotional, mental, and physical levels. Once we get through any "detox" stage, we start feeling better.

We acquire a new outlook, a new reference point. Thanks to your new, cleaner lifestyle, you'll begin to surprise friends and family with your new attitude. "Everything" gets better, because *you* get better.

The world is centered on your perspective, your point of view. A wholesome raw food regimen and other practices that lead to the purification of you, the center, will lead to greater harmony in the world around you. This new outlook also helps you to see new opportunities.

I look back on that age, 37. It was the moment *everything* started to change. I needed—desperately—some theme, some thread of positivity. My improved diet handed that to me.

How freeing can it be to include more raw fruits, vegetables, nuts and seeds in your diet? My prediction: Many problems will go away just by improving your diet. But that's only the beginning. You'll gain insight into an entirely new world of living.

As you increase the naturalness in one area of your life, you become, in various ways, a more authentic person. It's not unlike cleaning the clutter in your house—it makes you feel better in every way. It's entirely like getting out in the woods for a day in nature itself. *Everything* feels better.

My readers write to me that they get bewildered with so many different approaches to diets. It's hard to know what—and whom—to believe. *Great!* There's hope for the person who doesn't know what to believe. We need not believe anything at all. We need not hold to anyone's theory. We need to research, experiment, and understand. And do what *works* for us.

CHAPTER 12

You Already Have It!

You've doubtlessly read or at least heard of Napoleon Hill's 1937 masterwork, *Think and Grow Rich*, the best-selling self-improvement book *ever*. Fewer, though, have read Hill's *Outwitting the Devil: The Secret to Freedom and Success*.

This book was hidden from public view for more than seventy years. Too controversial, they thought. I wish I'd found and read it years ago—*Outwitting the Devil* is exactly the way-ahead-of-its-time sort of book I seek.

So what's with this whole "devil" thing? Hill's devil is certainly metaphorical. You might say his devil is the "negative side" of whatever you may be talking about. The opposite of confidence is fear. And for Napoleon Hill fear is the devil's main incarnation. His devil is the negative energy present in the mind of anyone who lives in fear.

Fear, says Hill, controls 98 percent of the population. It

grips us. It burns away our dreams and corrodes our confidence. It makes us abandon ambition in favor of the safe, the familiar. *I'd never make it... I couldn't do that... I'm too old... I'm not smart enough... What would people think?... No, that's silly...* Our excuses — translation: fears — are endless.

For Hill, hell is not a particular place, in the sense of 123 Elm Street or a neighboring galaxy. Yet, many people live there. Hell is fear. Heaven is inside us — as is hell, too. Hell is a state of being — not just a bad neighborhood, or some place south of here.

How did Hill get his "98 percent" figure? After interviewing some 25,000 people, he concluded: Only about two in a hundred had overcome their fears well enough even to formulate concrete goals for their lives. The rest were consumed in the negative. Immobilized.

Hill believed that people fall into drifting when they stop thinking for themselves, when they give up shaping their own lives. Without a determined destination, you're a drifter in a self-made hell. What's the way out? It is, Hill affirms, "the power of independent thought backed by definiteness of purpose."

I was definitely a drifter until my early forties. I kept earning degrees, but felt lost as to what to do with them. I was deeply unhappy. Unfulfilled.

My life changed the day I came across Lillian Müller's book, *Feel Great, Be Beautiful Over 40*, in which she shares her beauty secrets. Reading this book, I felt at a huge physical disadvantage compared with the author, a model since her teens. About the same time, my discovery of raw foods led to radically improved health and looks. Suddenly, the light dawned on me: Wouldn't it be all the more impactful if the author of a healthful lifestyle book could share how she'd succeeded, despite coming from great disadvantage, compared with most readers? I thought *That's it!* My *disadvantage* will become my *advantage*.

As soon as I started to form concrete goals, the bricks of my life began to fall into place. I stopped drifting. I had *purpose*.

I started reading books about how to write books. I was launched like a rocket into space. And I was happy. My husband didn't see it that way. Nick thought the whole thing was absurd. *Raw foods? Who'd buy a book like that? Are you dreaming? Get yourself a sensible business. Open a beauty shop... Try real estate... Use your degree and teach math!*

I stuck to my course. Nothing he or other relatives said would dissuade me. I was on the raw vegan diet, and that's what I wanted to write about. Intuitively, I knew what was needed to bring my goal to fruition: I must stay focused. And I must be true to myself.

In 2003 I published my first book, *Your Right to Be Beautiful: The Miracle of Raw Foods*. Later came more books, then beauty products. I've made a living doing what I love.

Thought first... *then* reality. Thoughts and emotions about possible experiences precede the physical manifestation of those experiences. Everything you're experiencing in the physical world right now is the net total of all the energetic vibrations that have found resonance with your most prominent past thoughts.

Things happen not so much *to* you as *through* you. Your physical experiences match your expectations — indeed, they were built by your expectations.

Don't try to figure out *how* your goal is going to come about. Your conscious mind will begin analyzing and scheming and calculating. If your mind doesn't come up with a satisfactory answer, you'll be flooded with doubts.

The best way to get rid of doubt is *not* to be in a terminal state of *want*, but instead in a state of living your dream.

Each experience corresponds to a particular bodily state. When you identify with a certain reality, you feel an accompanying sensation. When you're scared, your heart beats faster, you breathe more rapidly, and your body gets into that fight-or-flight state. When you receive an award, when you're typing the last paragraph of your new book, or finishing a marathon or a 5K race, you feel very distinct emotions. Upon achieving wealth and fame, there are certain bodily reactions as well. The body is your bridge between quantum possibility and physical experience.

For example, in 1998, I saw myself vividly being an author and having a successful business: helping women to improve their health and appearance. I *felt* my life then as I'm living it now.

I "knew" back then that Nick would "see the light" and actually start chewing celery instead of eating hamburgers and French fries, at least when I'm around. I even "saw" him taking charge of our shipping department. It happened almost exactly how I dreamed it. Yes, I'm still dreaming and I'm living my dream!

Recently, I watched an interview with a Russian best-selling detective novelist Tatiana Ustinova. She tells how she made up a detective for her novel, gave him a name, and described his appearance. Then, a year after the book was published, she met an actual, working detective with the *very same* name and an appearance much as she'd described. He'd never read her book, or she might have been in trouble!

When Ustinova attends readings and signings, she advises those of her fans who seek a romantic partner to write down, in as much detail as they can muster, how they "see" their ideal partner. They may not get a check from a publisher, but they will, sooner or later, says Ustinova, find that dream mate.

Whatever you *really* want, go ahead and write it down as if it's already happened, already materialized, already *there*.

A familiar expression—You want something so much you *can taste it*. Beyond merely formulating a goal, we have to envision it. See it. Hear it. Touch it. Focus on it. It's *then* our predominant feelings begin to align with the things and energies "out there" in the universe that can help us.

We create our reality not so much with the thoughts, but with emotions, that these thoughts generate. Every unique emotional frequency corresponds to a unique sensation that we feel. The moment you have a thought, it already exists as a quantum possibility. But to manifest it into your reality, you need to fuel it with energy, your emotion.

Consider this: If you could generate within your body the sensation, say, of owning a beautiful house, then you wouldn't be in the state of *needing* that house, would you? You'd have replaced the state of striving, wanting, and wishing—that somehow-maybe-someday feeling—with the mental state of having it, here and now.

Do you want a youthful, healthy body? Then you must begin *to feel* like a young, picture-of-health person. Tune your mental and physiological state to match how you'll feel when you're completely free of aches and pains and in tip-top shape. Start to behave as if you have it, as if it's happening today, right this minute.

Becoming that person in your thoughts is a sure way to materialize the youthful and vigorous you. You identify with that "imagined you" so completely, so totally, that you begin to behave as a fit and healthy person behaves. You'll keep to your exercise plan, and you'll watch what you're eating.

Want to be an entrepreneur? Simply picture that shop you wanted to open or that online home-based business you want to start. See it as a "done deal." Now, behave as entrepreneurs do.

Here's the main point: To bring something into your physical reality, you must feel you *already* have it. Take what you want as given, the same way you take each breath. Feel as if you've already arrived at your dream. See it: your fit body, your dream job, and your ideal life partner. And the best that will happen is the fear of failure vanishes. And you've made it into Hill's two percent!

CHAPTER 13

The Joys of Imperfection

Jail! For doing yoga? It almost happened... I saw the head-lines in my mind: BIONIC WOMAN FIGHTS FOR RIGHT TO DO YOGA...

The year was 2004. Bikram yoga came to town, and I de-cided to give it a try. I'll never forget that first class. My poses were all atrocious—balance nonexistent, stretching an agony. I even had to wipe away the odd tear from my cheek.

Worse, our instructor, the studio's owner, singled me out among thirty-some students. I'd explained my physical limita-tions to her before the class, but she still "corrected" my every move with callous delight.

For the tree pose, she had us bend the right knee and pull the sole of the right foot high upon the left thigh. Yow! I leaned my right foot on my left leg, just below the kneecap, thrilled to have gotten that far. "That is *not* the Bikram tree pose!" Her voice pierced the room, nailing me to the wall.

Look, I thought. *This crummy tree is the only vegetation you'll get from me today.* All I could say aloud was: "I can't do it."

"Hey!" she barked. "What's with the negative attitude?"

"I'll have to use a yoga strap to help me with the postures," I said.

"No modifications of poses allowed in my class," she insisted, adding icily that she'd rather get rid of me than compromise Bikram's sacred philosophy.

Negative attitude? Not me. If I'd had any doubts about coming to this yoga class again, they were gone now. *Better get used to it, lady. I'm here to stay!*

What she said next made my jaw drop.

"Take your strap and go, or I'll call the police and have you removed from the premises." By then she was on the phone, describing me to the cops. "Five-foot-nothing, dark hair, big mouth…"

A menacing description indeed. Imagining my picture smeared across the morning papers, I thought: *I hope they bring handcuffs.* (As an author, you just can't buy that kind of publicity.)

I suspect the response she got went something like this: "There's no law against bringing artificial body parts to class."

All night my hip muscles, beyond aching, burned. But next morning, walking felt *so* much easier. Yoga, I knew, was heaven-sent. I went to the second class. "Look," I told the owner. "You be nice to me, I'll come every day. You be mean to me… I'll come *twice* a day."

That's exactly what I did. I outlasted that owner, and kept going even after we moved away. I was the "worst" student in the class just about every time.

Being the worst is sobering, but also empowering. Giving myself *permission* to begin as the worst, I started Bikram yoga with only about 30% of the normal range of motion in my hips. I thought: *Ok, I'm at the bottom now, so the only way to go is up!*

To achieve anything worthwhile, adopt this attitude: Being the worst *is okay.* Indeed, deliberately putting yourself in such a state is necessary for real learning. Such humbling experiences can push you to excel in a way less challenging situations never could. You need to see how bad you are, so you will want badly enough to get better!

Be unafraid to look inadequate. Every time you find yourself in a situation where you're the worst of the bunch, I promise, it will give you a *strong* urge to improve.

Ballet has always fascinated me. Not the least reason is that ballerinas have such beautiful legs — the very attribute denied me in my youth. In 2012, a realization came to me: Ballet barre exercises must be very good for strengthening my hips and legs. I *had* to find a class.

I phoned every ballet studio in my area, hunting for adult ballet classes. I made a complete confession: *I'm 54, I've had eleven surgeries, and now I have two artificial titanium hips... Aren't you ready for somebody like me?"*

Their answers: *Ooohh, no... Sorry — that class has just filled up... Ah, no, you see the semester's already started.* Some, seeking to be merciful, were vague: *Don't think we have anything for you right now...* Others were dead blunt: *You wouldn't be able to keep up.*

Honesty, usually the best policy, was getting me no-where. I quit phoning. I simply *showed up* at a studio. In the AGE section on the form, I wrote "40+."

How does it feel to be in a class where you're forty years older — two generations — than nearly everyone else? As my instructor said later: *"Lady, you have guts."* Did I forget to mention that I showed up in black orthopedic shoes to balance my uneven gait, while everyone else sported pink ballet slippers?

Okay, so you have a dream. *Now* what? Will you make it a reality, or will it remain a mere fantasy? It's easy to simply hang around the house with your dreams. Fantasizing. Lingering. Loitering really, because you'd only be idle. *Goals*, not dreams, motivate you to action.

Fear of imperfection kills progress. It holds you back, deceives you, makes you procrastinate. Perfectionism isn't desire. It's fear. Fear of being inadequate, or of being *seen* as inadequate. Fear of being a failure.

Had I thought I could dance or do yoga only *after* resolving *all* my body issues, even by now, I wouldn't have started. Had I decided to wait until my English was perfect before writing books or blogs, or before giving a speech, there'd be no books, and you wouldn't be reading this now.

Seek the company of those who *have already achieved* what you want, doers who are farther along. Don't be intimidated by the gap you see. Indeed, the more gap between you and them, the better. When you *feel* that gap, your mind can make life-changing resolutions: *If Vicki wrote a book, so can I. Fred dances beautifully. If I keep practicing, I'll dance just as cleanly and gracefully as he does.*

You need what physicists call "potential difference" to

charge your desire, to propel mere wishful thinking toward an unstoppable drive that will bring your desires to life.

Practice doesn't make perfect. Practice reduces the imperfection.

— Toba Beta, *Master of Stupidity*

Do you feel less than nothing? Good. You see, you already have something in common with big achievers. If you want to match their success, you need to start where most of them started — at the bottom.

Many great achievers have been gripped by poverty, handicaps, or even by being outcasts. Such events can *make* you. They're precious for your soul, and your character.

They give you fresh perspective, wake you from lethargy, shove the truth in your face, and teach you what you should change. It's at such moments that your learning leaps forward. Such moments bring new ideas and fresh answers to lifelong questions that open up new avenues you'd never have thought possible.

These days, I often think of my first yoga teacher. I'd love to see her again. No, not to hand her an I-told-you-so. I'd rather give her a big hug and a huge expression of gratitude. Where would I be now, had she not given me that push? I'm so much better at yoga, now. She'd be proud of my postures, even my tree pose.

There will always be someone else who's better than you

at yoga. Someone will always be a better writer, dancer, singer, or accountant. Someone will always be prettier, younger, or richer. But there will never be another you. So be comfortable in being perfectly imperfect.

CHAPTER 14

Recreate Your Past!

My beginner's ballet class always starts with a 20-minute stretching session. The instructor's lithe and astonishingly flexible 17 year-old daughter, Megan, stood out among the students. As I was struggling with my poorly executed lunges, Megan dashed off perfect, graceful splits. I stared, captivated by the supple arch of her back and the flexibility in her hips.

Despite the severely restricted range of motion in my hip joints, I *so* much wanted to do a split. *I don't know how*, I thought, *but I'm going to do it.*

Then I was reminded of my doctors' advice, after my hip replacement surgeries: Don't try to do *anything* you couldn't do before. Before the operations I was primarily sitting—getting next to no exercise. Very little walking. That was my past, and they told me it had become my destiny. The clear implication: Don't plan on buying any ballet slippers.

The class started. When the instructor asked us to do a

split, I needed *two* of the five-inch blocks to place under the hamstrings of my forward leg. But in my mind, I was creating a different image: For my next book cover, I resolved to perform that full split. I even imagined the exact outfit in that cover photo and the way my hair would be braided.

Meanwhile, my progress crept along like a snail going up a hill, an extra-slow snail. Any rational observer would estimate a good 20 years for me to meet my goal — time I didn't have. Yet, my desire remained undiminished. I kept imagining myself doing the split exactly like Megan had done. But, for that to happen, my *past* had to change!

From a quantum physics prospective, that's not as far-fetched an idea as one might think. Consider a famous experiment — called Schrödinger's cat.

I'm against experimenting on animals, but philosophers call the experiment I'm about to describe, a *thought experiment*. So the only harm done pertains to stodgy old ways of thinking. Stick with me, please, as we follow the White Queen (of Lewis Carroll's *Through the Looking-Glass*) in believing "six impossible things before breakfast."

Physicist Erwin Schrödinger devised his thought experiment to demonstrate an apparent absurdity inherent in quantum mechanics. It goes like this: Imagine a box. We can't see or hear anything through its walls. In the box, there are three things: a cat… a flask of poison… and a mechanical device that will break the flask — but only if a certain subatomic particle decays — and releases the poison, killing the cat.

The only way we can tell whether the cat's alive at any moment is to open the box. Until then, quantum physics implies the cat is both alive *and* dead simultaneously. Even though the existence of the cat in the box *was* a reality, the alive-or-dead condition of the cat did not exist as a physical reality until it was perceived.

Here is the most remarkable part of Schrödinger's thought experiment: Let's assume the box is left alone for ten hours. Opening the box then and finding the cat alive creates a history of the past ten hours: the cat is very hungry, purring, and very glad to see you.

Opening the box and finding the cat dead now creates a very different picture of the past ten hours: The cat's body went stiff as rigor mortis set in, and its rigidity will give an indication of the hour of its demise.

In a sense, opening the box determines a *past* that did not exist until observed. (Somewhat similar to: *If a tree falls in a forest and no one is around to hear it, does it make a sound?*)

Can we, in real life, change the past? It turns out that we can.

Let me continue where I left off with my dream of executing a split… Soon after joining the beginner's ballet class, I met a massage therapist. I'll call her Lyndsey, age 29. She was also a tribal dance instructor.

Lyndsey, upon observing my movements, suggested a few exercises she thought might help. They did, and I asked her for more. Soon we started to meet for regular therapy sessions. Her knowledge of muscle isolation, of myofascial release techniques, coupled with her keen observation of my specific alignment needs, began to work wonders.

Within a month I tossed away my orthopedic shoes, having gained more and more flexibility in my hips. Most importantly, the unevenness in muscular development, that made my body looked crooked, began gradually to subside.

Three years later, I was doing a forward straddle-stretch, in which you're sitting on a mat, legs apart in a straddle position, while your torso bends all the way forward. Not quite a split, but it still seemed like a miracle to me.

Fine, you might say, but where is the promised "recreating your past?" I'm getting there. One day while working with Lyndsey, she asked, "Do you know that you have hypermobile joints?"

What? *Hypermobile* joints? I thought I had *immobile* joints. My hips were damaged at birth. Prolonged sitting and inactivity had created a big bulging tightness in my sacrum. My shoulders were uneven because of my limp. My elbow had been frozen—a medical condition where the elbow is locked in place—thanks to a bicycle accident.

No, I've never experienced what anyone would call *flexibility*, much less *hypermobility*. Then it dawned on me: Wait—my fingers! They've always been flexible.

What she said next blew me away. "Many people cannot do a full split, even if they exercise daily. But with your natural flexibility, Tonya, you will—and soon!"

Always remember that when you have committed yourself to an action, then the whole cosmos will conspire to help you. The key word is commitment.

— Mark Hedsel

Here's what happened. Napoleon Hill said it best: *Whatever the mind can conceive and believe, it can achieve.* If you hold a dream image in your mind, everything in your *past* and *present* will come forward to assist you, helping you materialize your dream.

As life and death were both present for Schrödinger's cat, everything you might ever wish is present in your life as a probability wave function. Actuality is determined by what's created by your desires.

I have a pretty good natural flexibility. But because of my injuries — and because of what I believed, and was taught to believe, about my limitations — I never knew about it for more than fifty years.

I might have wished to become a good singer (I'm wretched, actually), or to become a professor of mathematics (not so crazy a possibility, in my case). For an outside observer, my doing a split, under the circumstances, would have seemed an utterly unreal wish, since even the majority of young and fit adults can't do one. Yet, my past (as I knew it), was changed to accommodate my most daring dream.

The same thing happened when I decided to write my first book. I remember mentioning the idea to some of my American friends. They could barely resist laughing. They'd known me when I spoke broken English, having just emigrated from the former Soviet Union.

I had no prior experience in writing, except for getting a C in a creative writing course in high school. *Nothing* in my past would suggest writing as part of my career — neither I, nor anyone else, had seen any indication of this hidden talent. Yet, once I zeroed in on the wish to become a writer, something in my observed past began to change.

This time the revelation came from Ernest Hemingway — his biography. The famous author was asked *What does it take to become a writer?* His answer surprised me: "an unhappy childhood." Well, at least I had that requirement for being a writer. It turned out that what I had thought of as a negative was a positive.

My life is an endless well of ideas. And I pump it for all it's worth. I reached out to a terrific editor, Bradley, in my Toastmaster's club, whom I'd already known for several years. But I wasn't aware of his occupation before I put out the wish to become a writer.

Ever since, Bradley helped me not only "fix" what needs fixing in my work, but helped me learn more and more of the writerly arts. He's my literary Lyndsey, helping me exercise my writing muscles.

Quantum theory says there is no reality *until it's observed*, like Schrödinger's cat's whereabouts. Likewise, my exceptional flexibility, my remarkable editor and even my "good-for-writing" childhood, for all practical purposes, never existed until they were sought.

You're always free to change your mind and choose a different future or a different past.

— Richard Bach

I imagined. I saw in my own mind, the vision of a physically whole me, doing a split. I took action. And it happened —

just as I'd envisioned it. Well, almost. This book has a different cover, and I will be performing a *vertical* standing split for my next book cover *Living Ageless*. Close enough!

Quantum theory describes the unobserved physical world as being a superposition of potentialities. Similarly, *you* are a superposition of possibilities, doings and not-doings, good habits and bad habits, successes and failures. Just as a "look" would determine Schrödinger's cat's reality as either living or dead, your own "looking" for means to fulfill your dreams will help manifest them as realities.

Are there talents and abilities within you about which you've never known? You have, now, somewhere within you, *everything* you need to succeed in *any* endeavor. You have the potential to fulfill *any* of your dreams. The catch: *you must believe that it's possible!*

CHAPTER 15

How to Achieve the Extraordinary?

I f asked whether we could withstand an hour or longer encased in ice, most of us would say no. Indeed, were you or I to attempt it, we'd literally give up or die. A Dutchman, named Wim Hof, shows us the exception. As the holder of quite a peculiar record, Hof — popularly known as the Iceman — is able to stand, completely encased in ice, for up to one hour and fifty-two minutes, suffering no ill effects.

A genetic freak? That is *one* theory, though not an especially good one.

Hof, himself, doesn't claim any inherent ability at all. He attributes his remarkable capacity to simple — albeit long — training. It's training, he says, of the *mind*.

Similarly, Tibetan monks use a technique called Tummo to generate such high continuous body heat that they can spend a wintry Himalayan night sitting naked, wrapped in sheets dipped in ice-cold water, drying them with their body heat alone.

Each man imagines a blaze of fire at the base of his spine. Through deep concentration and deliberate breathing techniques, the monk causes the fire to extend all the way to the surface of his body to dry the sheets.

Dr. Herbert Benson, of the Benson-Henry Institute for Mind-Body Medicine at Massachusetts General Hospital, has studied this meditation practice. Benson and his team were amazed that these monks could raise their finger and toe temperature by as much as 17 degrees.

Less thoroughly researched, but reasonably well-documented incidents of walking through fire can be found in the book, *The Life and Teachings of the Masters of the Far East* by Baird Spalding. He was one of an 11-member research expedition traveling through India, Tibet, China, and Persia.

Spalding and his team found that practitioners who exposed themselves to fire and incurred no damage can do so by convincing themselves that they're not matter, but spirit. And of course, there's that fire-walking phenomenon — the exercise practiced at management training and self-empowering seminars. Participants walk across hot coals without getting burned by convincing themselves — their minds — that they can do it.

The core idea in these practices is that the world is created by the mind. In a very lively sense, quantum physics seconds this idea. Remind yourself about this constantly and you'll train your mind to become quantum-friendly.

Achievements are "impossible" only before they've been done. Mt. Everest, space travel, heart transplants, smashing weightlifting and running records, visiting the depths of the oceans — all these, we were told, were quite impossible. Somehow, they went from impossible to improbable to doable, and some feats even became commonplace.

Since 1997 I've been living a 100 percent raw food life-style, that hasn't been — not yet! — "proven" by nutritional and medical science to be beneficial for excellent health and youth-fulness. Some people even say it's an "impossible" lifestyle to maintain long-term. Yet, all the animals in nature do very well on raw foods, independently of scientific research.

When I first heard the raw food message, every fiber of my soul and body said: *This is so true.* I suppose you could call it a gut reaction. I resolved then and there to go raw. After more than 18 years on the raw food lifestyle, I made a significant dis-covery: Each of us gets a crack at something extraordinary in life. And we don't want to miss it.

Going raw was — and *is* — my extraordinary thing. It doesn't have to be yours. You'll know yours when you see it. Call it a "religious experience." A defining moment. A *Eureka* moment. An "Aha!" A light bulb coming on above your head.

You won't need any "proof" that it's the right thing to do. You won't need testimonials or textbooks. You'll just realize you've experienced a life-changing event.

Not once since going raw have I doubted my chosen life-style. I believed it would give me youthfulness and great flexi-bility in my "older" years, and it has. My unshakable belief as-sured my undeniable success.

I think it's an optimal way to eat, and a primary road to good health and youthfulness. Now, nutritional and medical scientists haven't *proven* that. This, however, doesn't worry me. It's rather like the implications of quantum physics. They work.

The experimental work on the raw food diet has barely begun. Reason: It's as hard to collect raw vegan eaters for a study than it is to collect most subatomic particles. There are a lot of linear accelerators around the world, but no laboratories dedicated to studying broccoli enthusiasts.

There are thousands of subscribers on my newsletter list who are interested in raw foods. Still, eating 100% raw foods is not for everyone. But it's not scientific tests that prove whether or not I—or you—can achieve something. It requires a special type of attitude, just as any real achievement does.

If you want to achieve greatness, stop asking for permission.

— Anonymous.

I once read about an 83-year old taking ballet classes. I never wondered what her doctor thought about it, whether her doctor approved, or thought it was silly or dangerous. I just wondered how I could be more like her.

When I saw a YouTube video of Matilda Klein ballroom dancing at age 94, I was blown away, and then baffled by the comment below: *How do we even know she is indeed 94?* You mean she might only be 91?

I decided: if these women can do it, so can I! Often, it's not an accomplishment or the final result that inspires me. Rather, it's the effort and the mindset that were essential to getting there.

One overwhelming reason we "can't" do things: *We don't try.* And, often, we don't try because we—along with everyone else—think it's impossible.

It's an insult to human nature to brand any feat as impossible. It's only a matter of time before someone does it. Nothing is out of reach. But, unfortunately, the mindset, *I can't do it* leads to: *Therefore, nobody else can.* The error in that thinking: *my* limitations are *everyone's* limitations. It becomes contagious — like the flu or the whooping cough.

Every man takes the limits of his own field of vision for the limits of the world.

— Arthur Schopenhauer, *Studies in Pessimism: The Essays*

Some would roll their eyes at those of us who want to claim in our physical, macro world the "superpowers" we have on the quantum level. But, the tiniest fraction of the physics community *does* see the connection between quantum theory and the law of attraction. The tiniest fraction of the medical community *does* see the value of raw foods in achieving health and slowing the aging process. And while my orthopedic surgeons left me in a wheelchair, one therapist was gutsy enough to take my case and succeed.

Go with the exceptions, not the expected. *Be* the exception.

What's "impossible" is determined only by the limits of your imagination. Anything can become a physical reality, but only if you dare to believe in it.

Your desires create your experiences. Those experiences, in turn, assure your growth and evolution. However daring your wish might be, don't trouble yourself with its claimed impossibility. The fact that you even want it means that it's *inside* your ring of possibilities.

How many of you have ever wanted to go to Mars? One-way, that is? I'm not going. There are a lot of experiences I don't want. I never had a desire to climb Mt. Everest or cross the Grand Canyon on a tightrope, like the Flying Wallendas. However, I wanted to dance, even though in my case, it looked "impossible."

We're all different, and that's a good thing. That's why others' desires often give us the reaction: *Why on earth would she want such a thing?* Our desires are unique to us. They help to shape our destiny. They are part of our identity, or we wouldn't ever want them.

You cannot have a strong desire for "the impossible." If you have a dream, it's a good indication you *can* achieve it. Go ahead! Elevate that thought from a mere idle dream all the way up to a goal. What you want already exists, is already happening, within the manifold layers of an infinite universe. Believe, visualize, and reach for the impossible, and see the extraordinary results unfolding before you.

CHAPTER 16

Young Goals... Great Expectations

You know this experience... You have to get up at 4 a.m. because your plane is leaving at 7 a.m. You set the alarm clock and the clock radio and even that little alarm on your cell phone. Then, about three minutes to four... Bingo! You're awake. No alarm yet, and, no, the dog didn't bark. It was your *intention* that awakened you.

Your mind was in charge. You told yourself you had to be up by four, and you made it happen. To put it another way: Your mind spoke... your body listened.

The same goes for solving any problem, big or small. Even losing weight, healing disease, or slowing the aging process. Activate that focused intention, and your body's cells and organs—all its faculties—will obey. The more intense, the more concentrated your intention, the better (and sooner) you'll succeed.

Focused intention will bring that necessarily different behavior and changed attitude. *Oh, I'll never lose that weight* becomes *Sure, I can.* Healthy people think healthy and act healthy. And that kind of thinking and action *brings* healthy living.

So, how much do our emotions, our expectations, or our talking about nutrition and anti-aging practices affect our health and apparent age? Answer: *a lot.*

We ourselves are observers, and through our own individual perceptions we create and influence what we see as the "real" world. What we observe appears to depend upon what we *choose* to observe.

Just as we vigorously defend our religious and political beliefs, we are as headstrong about the beliefs we have regarding our own bodies. As for aging, most believe they *must* become decrepit and die at a certain age. Society continually etches these beliefs in their brain.

Handsome, and only 38 years old — that was my father-in-law when I first met him. Yet he was always referring to himself as "old." The Bible verse he quoted most was Psalm 90:10: *The years of our life are seventy, or even by reason of strength eighty; yet their span is but toil and trouble; they are soon gone, and we fly away.*

Once I pointed out the verse Genesis 6:3: *Then the Lord said, My Spirit will not contend with humans forever, for they are mortal; their days will be a hundred and twenty years.* My father-in-law would argue that it is "his" verse — the first quoted above — that's relevant for our time.

It looked to me that my father-in-law never wanted to live long. He fully expected to get sick and feeble. He became blind and fragile several years before his death at 69.

Argue for your limitations, and sure enough they're yours.

— Richard Bach

On the other hand, those who have lived long lives usually wanted to do so.

Case in point: the Soviet ballerina Marina Semyonova was determined to live to be 100. Why? When Semyonova danced in *Giselle* at the Paris Opera in 1935, former Polish-Russian prima ballerina, Matilda Kshesinskaya, was the only one among the Russians in Paris who did *not* attend and pay her respects.

Matilda died four months short of her 100th birthday. Semyonova couldn't help but notice the snub and determined to outdo her rival by living to 100. And she did, making it almost to 102.

I'm sure you have met people who have expressed a similarly strong desire to reach their centenary, and who have gracefully reached that benchmark.

Those who teach the young, who work and play with youths, often live long productive lives. If you don't happen to teach classes to younger people, why not take classes with a young bunch?

I take beginner's ballet classes with a flutter of young girls. It's amazing how "anti-aging" it feels. And, indeed, "anti-gravitational," too! Hang with the young, and soon you'll feel yourself — at first imperceptibly, then quite consciously — taking on their posture, their facial expressions, even their vocabularies and vocal energies.

Your grandchildren may or may not do the trick. Plenty of over-fifties look forward to their children producing offspring so they can dote upon their grandkids. But if you become the built-in-babysitter, if you're merely entrusted with looking after the little darlings' needs, as too many seniors do, you may miss the "youthening" effect all together. Aim higher, much higher!

Wishing to live to see your grandson receive his college diploma is one thing, but how about wishing to run a marathon with him to celebrate his graduation?

We age because we stop having goals that require us to have a young body. The body then responds by giving up its capabilities for performing "young" tasks.

You are what you eat—everybody knows that. But you are, also, what you expect.

I eat healthful food. I exercise. But the main reason I stay youthful is because I have long decreed to my body: *You'd better be ready to dance when I'm done with restoring the mobility in my hips, whatever age that will be.* I told my body many times: I am *not* giving up my childhood dream to dance, and dance freely and have others see it.

It is crucial to convince your mind that you *are* getting healthier and more vigorous. If you find this hard to believe, consider: Whatever we cannot believe, we cannot experience. So, if you are not getting younger with age, it's only because you don't believe it's possible. Yet, it *is* in your power to change your beliefs, so your currently perceived limitations concerning your body will become obsolete.

Develop the firm conviction that simply growing older chronologically need not affect your body in negative ways. The secret of creating this reality lies in our attitude. It follows that a person who doesn't believe in aging will not age.

What are your "young" desires? Goals are essential for you to stay healthy and youthful. And they'd better be challenging goals as well. The body has to be healthy and youthful *for a good reason*.

If you don't plan to run like a young adult at sixty, you'll never be able to do it. Your body will release you from any ability your mind lets go of, thinking you don't need it any more.

If you don't plan to climb a mountain at eighty, why would you have strong legs? If you don't plan on doing a belly dance solo at ninety, why would you need a slim waist? Your body will not let you keep anything you don't plan to use and don't use daily.

Do others have to think your goals are right or reasonable? Not at all. For example, now I have goals such as getting good at tribal and spiritual dance, doing challenging yoga postures, writing a historical novel about my favorite ancient philosopher Pythagoras. I have other super-ambitious goals—some so hot I won't risk writing them here, lest they burn the paper.

It's okay that some of these goals are as far away as the moon. It's okay that friends and acquaintances gasp at my audacity—I've been there before. It doesn't matter what others deem impossible. I believe that I *can* accomplish them. That's all that's needed, and I'm only 58!

The best part... your body will be listening to your outrageous expectations and will do everything needed to keep up, helping you fulfill them.

Here's the best anti-aging recipe: Allow yourself to harbor "young" desires and plans, and your body will have no choice but to cooperate. *Expect* your body to stay young... make sure it understands... and it *will* perform according to your greatest expectations.

CHAPTER 17

Get Obsessed!

I was looking, in my writing, for the best analogy to explain the state of mind we'd need to invite extraordinary events into our life. Just then, an email rolled in, a *harrumph-harrumph unsubscribe* from my monthly newsletter...

I like Tonya's books and the website is good, but it seems TZ is OBSESSED. There's a difference between obsessed with being more youthful and simply being passionate about it.

Thank you! That's it! Yes! I'm obsessed! And overjoyed to be so. By definition, *obsession* is "an idea or thought that continually preoccupies or intrudes on a person's mind."

That's how discoveries are made. Albert Einstein, when asked how he got his brilliant ideas, answered that it was "curiosity, obsession, and dogged endurance."

That's also how world records are broken and art masterpieces are created. Wayne Gretzky didn't become a great player by being "somewhat interested" in hockey. Rembrandt didn't become an iconic artist by taking a few Tuesday night classes down at the community center. Hemingway didn't just scribble out a few ideas when they popped into his head. These giants in their fields were *obsessed*.

I was watching a movie, *The Gabby Douglas Story*, a biopic about the first black gymnast to win the individual Olympic All-Around Championship. Here's what she said: *You want to know how to become a champion? It's easy. Turn your dream into your goal. Plant it deep in your heart, then for the next ten years eat, sleep, breathe, laugh, and cry without ever taking your eye off your goal.*

It takes time to learn to dance—much longer when you have a set of titanium hips. (And you set off the alarms at the airport.) I want—I'm determined—to feel and look *fabulous* by the time I've become a good dancer. It might take another few years. I've just turned 58, so the clock is ticking. Still, I have no doubt I'll make it. How? "Obsession and dogged endurance."

There *are* unhealthy obsessions, no doubt. If you're so into playing video games that you forget about going to work, or picking up the kids after school, or feeding the dog, or taking care of the baby… there's a problem, and a serious one.

But there's nothing more uplifting in life than having a positive obsession, one that brings real meaning to your life. Such an obsession enables you to overcome enormous obstacles and perform extraordinary feats. *Mountain? What mountain? Are you talking about that molehill over there?*

It's as if you're vibrating at an especially creative frequency. You feel capable of collapsing the "wave of probability" in whatever you're obsessed with, bringing it into a physical reality.

Emotions are a driving force in any creative process. Everything with which you're preoccupied, everything that dwells in your mind and heart, can result in a physical manifestation. What begins as an obsession—a merely mental thing—becomes reality.

While getting ready for a visit from our friends, we decided to replace our old, worn-out fence. What type should we get? I decided I'd have a look on my way to the local grocery store, just to see what types of fences there were on that six-mile route.

Wow! Thirteen distinctly different kinds of fences, just on our block! I couldn't believe it. I'd driven this very same way, daily, for several years, and I'd never seen those fences before. Never really looked. I paid them no attention. Fences just hadn't been on my radar. Now I'm seeing fences *everywhere*, in all their myriad varieties. If the matter weren't so trivial, we could say I became "obsessed" with fences.

What you *focus on* is what you'll *find*.

In the world unified by the new physics, anything you could ever wish for already exists as a possibility. In quantum mechanical terms, the creation of something in the material world happens precisely when an observer, by the very act of observing, collapses a wave-possibility function into a particle. What does this "observing" mean? It means giving *deliberate attention* to something.

Were we living in that super-micro world, we'd be able to walk through walls, go back in time, and transport ourselves instantly to any part of the world or beyond. We would never get sick, nor would we age, and we could bring anything we wished into being. We'd have, in short, "superpowers." Everything, including us, is made of quantum material. So why can't we do all these things?

Since the birth of quantum mechanics decades ago, physicists have endeavored to unravel this mystery. How is it that all this quantum strangeness works on the subatomic level, but seems to disappear when we're getting to bigger things?

A currently popular theory explains why all the possibilities available at the quantum level do not appear in the material world around us. It's called the *decoherence theory*. Here is a grossly simplified account of the process by which a quantum possibility becomes reality...

Imagine you're observing a coffee cup. Before interacting with the environment, a system — a cup — is in all possible states at once. Decoherence theory suggests that you are not the only observer. The environment itself is also an active observer. *Environment*, in this case, is every*one* and every*thing* around an observed object. You're observing that cup, and so is everyone and everything else.

When your cup interacts with the environment, *superselection* is realized and the most stable state materializes. That state becomes robust and stable when a *lot* of information about the object — the most intense energy — is stored in the object's environment.

The main challenge in creating a quantum computer is to create a stable state in which an object has no interaction with the environment. Researchers are working to achieve the near-absolute zero temperature at which such a system would operate. For our practical purposes, however, eliminating the environment is impossible.

Consider your own goals. Remember that the environment is a bigger player in phenomena, more often than we are.

It takes more than *your* attention to reach a goal. Others out there in the general environment—and that environment itself—must be convinced you can do it.

Let's say you have the goal of writing a book. You'll become *very* knowledgeable in your chosen subject. You'll read everything available. You might want to take writing classes or find a good editor. You'll write every day. You'll constantly discuss your topic with well-informed individuals who can critique your work or help you generate new ideas. You'll query agents or publishers diligently. And you'll find one. If need be, you'll start your own publishing company.

Think those things, talk those things, focus on those things, and you'll be convincing yourself, others, and the world at large that you being a published author is an attainable "stable state" for the system—*you*—to occupy.

It is your intense interest—your behavior as you already have it, your *focus*—that collapses energy into physical reality. In a way, it's your obsession that will "convince" your environment that you're, in fact, a published author.

There *is*, indeed, as my email correspondent reminds us, a difference between being *obsessed* with an idea and being *passionate* about it. If you're passionate, you can accomplish *some*thing. But if you're obsessed, you can achieve *any*thing.

My advice: Make the car payments! Take care of your kids! Obey the law! Wash the dishes! But beyond that, go ahead: *Become obsessed* about the life you want. Get seriously immersed in your dream!

Become obsessed about the things you want. Otherwise you are going to spend a lifetime being obsessed with making up excuses as to why you didn't get the life you wanted.

— Grant Cardone

CHAPTER 18

The Key to Fearless Living

Mother did it! The look on my friend's face spoke a dozen emotions—none of them good. Lisa slammed the car door. That's when I saw the monstrous multi-legged spider-like crack across the windshield.

Lisa had phoned to say she'd be coming for a visit with her husband, Bob, and her mother, Eileen. I was standing in the driveway when they pulled in, Bob driving, with Lisa beside him, and her mom in the backseat.

I learned that during their ride, Lisa was knitting, relaxed with her feet up on the dashboard. Eileen was concerned about this position being unsafe. She became increasingly agitated. *Lisa, listen... If Bob has to brake suddenly...* but Lisa wouldn't budge. *Please, Lisa, listen...* Eileen persisted. *You could end up going through that windshield...* More fret, more urgency each time.

You can see it coming... another car abruptly changes lanes and suddenly slides in front of Bob. He slams on the brakes, tires screeching. Lisa's feet slip... press against the windshield... the glass cracks.

Now, it's not illegal to put your feet on the dash, but trauma doctors can tell you horror stories on this topic. Luckily, Lisa got away with only bruised knees.

Call Eileen's reaction reasonable worry. Call it premonition. I call it a vivid example of how we create our reality. Eileen's fear was palpable. Her fear put her in a horrified emotional state, as if the worst had *already* happened. Lisa played her part, too. She was defiantly careless, and contemptuous of her mother's worry and emotional state. Both mother and daughter invited, even created, the event itself.

Fear is our most basic instinct — key to our survival. Fear saves us, but it can also prey on us, stealing the very life it seeks to protect.

Readers of my books are health-conscious, so I often receive emails expressing concern about our environment: We live, one reader said, in a "terribly toxic world."

True. It's nigh impossible to avoid GMO foods, laced with antibiotics, additives, and insecticides. Pollution runs rampant, affecting water supplies everywhere. And, we face unprecedented levels of electromagnetic radiation.

Once, consumers didn't differentiate between an apple and a piece of candy, between mother's milk and baby formula, between lead-based powders and "natural" cosmetics. Since then, we've learned the benefits that healthful eating bestows on our wellness and looks. We know what happens on the molecular level when we eat GMO foods or food grown with pesticides. We're careful about what we eat, and what we put on our skin. And in most cases, this awareness helps to keep us healthy.

Still, there are exceptions. We've all seen them. There's that gal who eats only organic food, super-careful about everything that goes into or touches her body. Every morning, she dutifully works out in the gym. Yet, suddenly, she gets sick. Now, take that guy, who downs burgers and steaks regularly, bypasses the organic food in the supermarket because he "couldn't be bothered," still smokes half a pack of cigarettes a day and calls that "cutting down." Yet, he seems to press on in robust health way into his 90s. And we're left to wonder: How can that be?

This story might explain...

In the aftermath of the 1986 nuclear disaster in Chernobyl, most locals were resettled, but some 1,200 returned. Most died. Remaining, however, to this day, is a group of older women, living in a zone severely contaminated by radionuclides.

This Zone of Alienation is more heavily contaminated than any other region on Earth. These women drink contaminated water and milk and eat the meat of contaminated animals, but they've stuck it out for thirty years. When authorities tried to roust them, their response was: *Forget it! We're not moving.*

Today, with many in their eighties and nineties, these women express remarkable attitudes: *I only think about the good things in life.* One woman reportedly said, *Why should I be afraid of radiation? It doesn't bite!* Interesting fact: When some of these women did die, the causes were not cancer from radiation, but more often from heart disease—the most common cause of death for women everywhere.

They've simply never believed in the danger of radiation.

They couldn't see it, so, for these hardscrabble, salt-of-the-earth folks, it didn't exist.

It's not ignorance, of course, that fuels this remarkable survival story. It's spirit.

Medical science can't readily explain it. Quantum physics might. The new physics reveals: The nature of reality depends on the observer. No observer, no reality. The observer influences reality, or "creates" it.

Your focus, quantum physics instructs, can collapse a probability wave. Believe you're surrounded by poison ... and it will become your reality. When we concentrate on toxins, we *ready* ourselves to receive them. But, focus on health, maintaining a positive attitude, and you're actively helping your body to deal with its environment and to cleanse itself.

On one Internet forum, a man was sharing his nightmare—the endless illnesses he's developed because he's become highly sensitive to electromagnetic frequencies. *I hate wireless*, he exclaimed. What he's really saying is: He *fears* wireless. Could it be that his "hating" contributes to, even attracts, the very sickness he's experiencing?

What we hate or fear, we attract. Can we really control the emotions that rise within us? Not instantly. But we can control the beliefs that bring us negative emotions. This is *learned* behavior. Repeatedly undo the causes of negative emotions on a conscious level, and it will gradually become a subconscious routine.

You fear something. There's nothing you can do to prevent it. So what now? Imagine events unfolding in a safe, productive, even enjoyable way. Focus on that. *Feel* it! Feel the event happening. Feel yourself coming through unscathed. Feel within yourself a gratitude for it, happening the way you want it, and you *will* get through it.

Eat organic food whenever you can. Cleanse your body regularly. Know what you put on your face and body. But do not be afraid of what you cannot control. Think of those Chernobyl babushkas, living against all odds, all poisons, on love. Love of the land they couldn't leave.

The time has come to look even deeper, and beyond the molecular level. On the quantum level, a poison and a beneficial nutrient are just electrons and protons, neutrons, plus other particles. Go layers deeper, beneath the particles. Mass disappears, and all you have is *energy*. Have loving thoughts and you'll put yourself in a state of love. We don't know exactly how it works, but one thing is obvious: love is a potent antidote.

"I ain't never scared." This is a gutsy attitude, especially coming from someone in the centenarian crowd. Doris Long, age 101, is the oldest *abseiler* in the world. What's an abseiler? It's a person who descends from very high vertical structures on ropes.

Doris started abseiling at age 85. Since then, she and her descending events have raised money for charity sixteen times. A July 18, 2015 article in London's Daily Mail documents: Doris has rappelled down the 560 feet of Britain's tallest building, and she wants to beat her own record next year.

When I looked at her face in the newspaper photos and the web video, I couldn't help noticing that she wears an expression on her face not unlike those Chernobyl babushkas: trustful, peaceful, loving. As if they know something the rest of us don't. These unflaggingly young oldsters expect no harm. And they don't get it.

Sure enough, Doris's own words confirmed my impression: "I don't feel afraid and never have, I just have a placid nature."

Much of *my* life I lived by this credo: Keep a good heart —the worst is yet to come. And, oh! The worst *did* so often come. I feared everything. Illness. Injury. Financial ruin. Living in fear was making me deeply unhappy.

Lately, I've been living differently. I'm *not* fearless yet. Occasionally, fearful thoughts still come. When fear does creep in, I stop what I'm doing. I acknowledge it. I say, mentally or aloud, with all the self-assurance I can muster: *I'm trusting life. I'm learning willingly. I'm showing no resistance. And all is well. And it shall be.* I mean every word of this self-affirmation. Corny? A little weird? Sure. But it *works*. Try it and see for yourself!

CHAPTER 19

Death Is Not a Problem ...

The root of all fears: the fear of death. Everything you fear — ill health for you, loss of a loved one, fear for your career — derives from the fear of death.

Death is always imminent, whether the result of a zombie apocalypse or a slip in the shower. But that's not the real problem. The *fear* of death is the culprit. And, as with any illness, the best approach is to address its *cause*, not the outward symptom.

Some people have lived through "near-death experiences" (NDE) of one sort or another. Some have met "clinical death" on the operating table and came back. The experience became a turning point for them.

At one time, NDEs were strictly fodder for supermarket tabloids (not to mention a long string of zombie movies). Your standard tabloid NDE involved bright lights, angelic figures, and claimed messages from the beyond. We wrote these visions off as hallucinations, or as the imaginative products of a few publicity seekers' intense desire to appear in the papers.

The situation has changed. Since the seventies, ever-wider use of developing, and more daring resuscitation techniques, have enabled doctors to bring back ever-growing numbers of cardiac arrest patients. Rather than a few oddities, we now have literally millions of NDE cases.

We've known since about 2007 that, under some conditions, brain cells can remain alive for hours after standard vital signs cease. As a result, patients are pulled back after being "out there" for hours, not just minutes.

Medical science has thus given us a whole new breed — and quite a population of them — who have glimpsed beyond the veil.

Those who've visited the edge and returned, range in gender, ethnicity, religious creed, intellect and education. They come from laborers and homemakers to heart surgeons. Across these spans, person after person reports: There *is* life after death. There *is* a spiritual world beyond. And the world they've experienced was so often reported to be replete with love, light, and compassion.

Death when unmasked shows us a friendly face and is a terror only at a distance.

— Oliver Goldsmith

Dr. Eben Alexander, a neurosurgeon, was originally a big skeptic about near-death experiences, believing them to be simply fantasies, hallucinations produced by brains under extreme stress. He so believed until one day, at age 54, he contracted *E. coli* meningitis. The bacteria were eating up his brain. He spent 7 days in a coma—"brain dead."

But he came back. Thereafter, his mental abilities, far from being impaired, were notably enhanced—the case with most NDEs. He then wrote his best-known work, *Proof of Heaven: A Neurosurgeon's Journey into the Afterlife*. There's no shortage of books and articles on the subject by all manner of those who've lived through NDEs. But here was one, at last, by a scientific *insider*.

Dr. Alexander considers each hypothesis one by one that his colleagues, and he himself, in former days, would offer to explain accounts of experiencing the afterlife. Mind had been reduced to brain, for both science and philosophy. But, now, Dr. Alexander had come to characterize this view as one of "transparent flimsiness," a Kepler-esque fighting to preserve the scientific status quo.

His principal conclusion: Mind and consciousness *cannot* be reduced to brain activity. And God cannot be reduced to an angry old man with huge power, and an even bigger ego: He wants to be worshipped, and will punish us if we do not obey.

One of Dr. Alexander's thoughts has registered especially strongly with me: "Much—in fact most—of what people have had to say about God and the higher spiritual worlds has involved bringing them down to our level, rather than elevating our perceptions up to theirs. We taint, with our insufficient descriptions, their truly awesome nature." In other words, we humans must stop making God *less*, by creating Him in *our* image.

Increasingly, the evidence of near-death experiences reveals that death is a portal to an afterlife and that the universe is guided by a vast, unconditionally loving intelligence. God is indeed love, nothing but love, without beginning or end. And this is good news. No longer can the implications of NDEs be ignored by physics, by medicine, or by churches.

Death is for many of us the gate of hell; but we are inside on the way out, not outside on the way in.

— George Bernard Shaw

I don't recommend *seeking* the near-death experience. There's a bus figuratively waiting to run over each of us — no point looking up the schedule to meet it. But reading about such experiences will expand your worldview immensely.

Despite all the differences they exhibit, NDEs tend to feature some strong commonalities: a feeling of separation of consciousness from the physical body... intense and generally positive emotions... the impression of passing into or through a tunnel... seeing a mystical, often brilliant light... encountering initial greeters, either angelical beings or deceased loved-ones... a review of one's life. Often, people returning from NDEs recount "other realms," and gaining access to some kind of special knowledge.

Even though most NDE survivors describe their near-death experience in "heavenly" terms, for some, their over the veil voyage was anything but pleasurable.

Noted NDE authority, P.M.H. Atwater, wrote her well-known book *Near-Death Experiences* after interviewing some 4,000 individuals who had survived clinical death.

She sought to find connections between the survivors' prior beliefs and what they had really experienced during their NDEs. Atwater found that the beliefs a person held prior to an NDE do indeed influence the kind of experience the person will have in the "other realm."

She noted a certain pattern. What a person experiences is whatever he or she is *capable* of receiving. Beings, forms, and feelings one finds in an NDE correspond to one's capacity to accept them.

For example, some adults experience a loving family reunion, or reassuring religious figures, or "light beings," breathtaking landscapes. Before the incident, these adults valued life and family ties, believed that every good deed counts, and that helping others will be rewarded.

Others, however, endure a distressing experience, describing an encounter with a threatening void, or agonizing purgatory, "hauntings" from their past, or having to face unfinished business. People who usually report such experiences have held in deeply suppressed guilt, fear, and anger, before the NDE event. They had been living with the expectation of some kind of punishment or discomfort after death. And their NDE visions usually matched their expectations.

And there are those individuals, Atwater finds, who, prior to their NDE, were always ready for challenges, for opportunities to stretch their minds. These people often report encounters with otherworldly "higher dimensions," and receiving visions and revelations of some great truth.

These aren't sharply drawn categories, as you might expect. One kind of NDE can shade into another. But all who have gone through NDEs have received what they needed for their souls' expansion, facing issues integrated within the deepest self. It sure looks like we create our own reality, even after death.

The fear of death follows from the fear of life. A man who lives fully is prepared to die at any time.

— Mark Twain

While working on this chapter, I was rereading Plato's account of Socrates' death. There was no fear — instead, a hint of enthusiasm, the thrill of a person who had learned all he could in life and was about to learn something new. We hear, through Plato, Socrates' last words: *The hour of departure has arrived, and we go our ways — I to die, and you to live. Which to the better fate is known only to God.*

No matter the cause of death, the suffering that may have preceded it, the moment of death itself is pleasurable. Death has one important aspect in common with love: Both happen "in the moment," and whatever happens in the here-and-now has the capacity to bring the purest bliss. (However, most people are not in a hurry to find it out!)

At a recent funeral, my relatives crying over the deceased reminded me of an evocative metaphor about death in regard to the metamorphosis of a butterfly.

Does the caterpillar think it dies to become a butterfly?

In its caterpillar phase, it does nothing but eat 24/7. When it finishes growing, it rests in its chrysalis phase, while at the same time developing into an adult butterfly. Could the worm-like caterpillar have imagined its new colorful, freely flying butterfly life? It's the same with the human embryo, living within and then leaving its mother's womb. It doesn't *want* to come out, it doesn't want, in effect, to be born.

Perhaps it's the same when we die. We don't want to die… but perhaps we're missing out, in such thinking, on contemplating the transition to a whole new kind of existence.

We don't have to go through near-death experience, to realize: It's only when we eliminate the fear of death that we can begin living.

Death is not extinguishing the light; it is putting out the lamp because the dawn has come.

—Rabindranath Tagore

CHAPTER 20

Who Art Thou, Lord?

English is my second language. I work with editors all the time. I've noticed that even accomplished translators and editors tend to change the text according to their *own* knowledge and experience, to further their *own* beliefs.

In my case, often the corrections and additions are very helpful and do clarify the point I'm making, but on some occasions they introduce a meaning opposite to my original intent.

We all do this constantly. Words mean different things to different people. Each of us assigns a "story" to a word, some special context or set of personal beliefs, to an event or an object we encounter. We bring this "story" to whatever we do, whether we tell, write, translate, or interpret it. We always assign meanings that correspond to our feelings, understanding, and personal experiences.

Editorial mishaps are not a big deal in my case. I'm not that important, plus I'm alive and well and in a position to make immediate adjustments. Having witnessed my own ideas changed by editors, and much more so by translators, to the extent of conveying the opposite of my intended meaning, I began to ponder on how spiritual writings of the past may have been distorted by scribes and translators through the ages. If the text's concepts are beyond a scribe's or a translator's ken—you're bound to get a lot of contradictions.

It's obvious that elevated minds throughout history have known—though under other names and brands—some of the key elements of quantum mechanics: There is unity among all things.

Philosophers and mystics have talked about universal connectedness for millennia. Quantum theory now clearly lends strong support to this concept of universal connectedness through quantum *entanglement*.

In classical physics, two physical systems could exist that were utterly distinct, so that nothing that happened in one could affect the other. Nothing that happens in Cleveland, say, would affect what goes on in Sacramento. In classical Newtonian physics, they had *separability*.

Now, enter the microscopic world. What goes on with a particle here does affect what goes on with one over there. And sometimes, *way* over there, with no levers or pulleys in between. No anything. It's downright counterintuitive. Einstein himself called it "spooky action at a distance." The trouble for Newtonian physicists is: Too many experiments prove it really does happen.

University of California physicists in 2009 demonstrated a quantum entanglement between two objects big enough to see with the naked eye. Quantum theory sets no limit on the size of the objects. Indeed, researchers agree: The only limitation on their observing large-scale quantum phenomena is budget.

No more separability. What we have instead is *entanglement*. One particle can, it seems, instantly affect another at a distance, without mechanical interaction.

When two particles or systems are entangled, it's like a long-distance romance. Though they're in two cities, what happens to one somehow gets translated into an effect on the other. And it happens instantaneously.

All—you and I and everything else—are parts of a unified, causally connected whole. We are all interconnected and the idea that "I" am an entirely separate physical entity is an illusion. *Nonseparability* is now the order of the day.

Our perception of God is also changing, thanks (among other factors), to quantum theory. We no longer need to think of God as a force or a being entirely separate from ourselves, or from the rest of the universe.

The Newtonian world was a clockwork universe. Within it, God was viewed as a wise clockmaker, the fellow who wound up the clock—the universe—and let it operate according to preset laws. In the new quantum universe, God is no longer a distant, disconnected personage.

Consider... If God were entirely separate from us, and from the universe, that would mean God has boundaries. God would not, then, be omnipresent. The major religions believe God *is* omnipresent. Arguably, then, quantum theory's implications, while dissolving some of our precious images of God— the old man on the throne, for example—essentially deliver God more in tune with fundamental beliefs—including that God is "everywhere."

How we see God often says more about us than about

anything in the spiritual realm. We humans are always in the business of "making" gods. An ancient thinker once said: "If rams and goats could beget a god, he would have horns." We're doing the same thing... We create God in *our* image.

You can safely assume you've created God in your own image when it turns out that God hates all the same people you do.

— Anne Lamott, American novelist

We cast God, so often, in human terms. We attribute to God distinctly human emotions—as needing praise and devotion, as having regrets and being vengeful, as getting lonely and having loyalties. We project our own perceptions on the Higher Power. Such perceptions are often individualized: To a kind person, God seems kind and loving, while a jealous person sees God as jealous, even vindictive.

The Aramaic word for *God* means, variously: *sacred unity... oneness... the all... one without opposite... ultimate power or potential*. Only oneness is real, says this word, and quantum physics points in the same direction: Separability is an illusion.

However, our minds cannot easily comprehend universal connectedness. Why? Because our minds, in themselves, are finite. The human mind operates on subject-object relations: You, the *subject*, perceive the *object*.

Now hear Erwin Schrödinger, Nobel Prize winner in physics: "Subject and object are only one. The barrier between them cannot be said to have broken down as a result of recent experience in the physical sciences, for this barrier doesn't exist."

Now, imagine a deeply spiritual person who has experienced quantum entanglement through meditation or other spiritual practices, who knows that separability is an illusion, who knows he is one with God, and who shares his experience with others. When there are no words for it, how can he explain it?

Jesus largely spoke Aramaic. Like all human languages, it's an imperfect vehicle of communication. His words were translated to Greek, to Latin, to English, and to a myriad other languages. Many translations have not been done directly from the original language, and have used Latin or even English as base languages.

If you haven't seen *KJB — The Book That Changed the World*, I strongly recommend you watch this extraordinary documentary on how the most powerful translation of the Bible emerged. King James believed that a single "authorized version" would unite the conflicting factions of the Church of England and the Puritans, whose enmity was tearing apart both church and country.

A committee of fifty clergymen and scholars were charged with a task of producing the most complete and accurate translation of the Bible. King James set dozens of hard, specific rules the translators had to follow. For example, when a meaning is hard to understand, make it "agreeable" to common people.

Among King James's directions to the English translators were the following: "When any word hath divers significations, that to be kept which has been most commonly used by the most eminent fathers, being agreeable to the propriety of the place, and the analogy of the faith."

This is very significant, because most commonly used meanings are all about duality, *people* and *things* being regarded as separate. The translators were the most capable translators of all times. But they too, like all of us, were held by the mind's two-part view of reality and had no concept of the unity of all things.

Consequently, many of the Bible's writers, scribes, translators and commentators, unaware of the principle of nonseparability, endeavored to make the text more comprehensible by adding their own clarifications.

That is how God comes across in many biblical and other religious texts as a separate entity. That is how the "Kingdom of Heaven" ends up as a place or quasi-place, as a distinctly bordered parcel of real estate.

In the first book of John, chapter 1, verse 5, we read: *God is light; in Him there is no darkness at all.* The addition of *Him* represents, I believe, our inability to dissociate from the mind-produced dualism of subject and object.

The Image of God is your final obstruction to a religious experience.

— Joseph Campbell

God cannot be explained. And God cannot be a "He" or a "She," strictly considered—capital letters notwithstanding, because *He* and *She* imply *someone else, a third person.* This is why many people try to find another word, another signpost that

140

points to this entity we so inadequately call *God*. Some use words like *Universe* or *Source*. Neither is apt, because they, too, carry the implication of being *object* — separate, that is, from you, from us.

The best word for God (even though it may take some time getting used to) is one Jesus used: God is Love. God is neither object nor subject. God is, then, a state of being, a state that the word *Love* expresses best.

I like to add *Infinite Love*, to differentiate it from romantic or parental love, to show the love we're talking about is everlasting and all encompassing.

The illusion that you are separate from God is subtle but strong and makes one feel small, helpless, and afraid. However, the separability principle that classical physics took for granted — in accepting the illusion our senses impose on us — is totally invalidated by the implications of quantum mechanics. Indeed, the realization that there is no separation is part of what is called *enlightenment*.

Wikipedia defines *enlightenment* as "full comprehension of a situation." A better definition, perhaps: a full comprehension of reality. Enlightenment is seeing things as they are, rather than as they appear.

To get out of a locked room, we need first to realize that we're trapped in it. If we worry about our health, if we fear for our children, if we're concerned about losing our job, whatever the problem may be, our first step is to realize that we're not living in a state of bliss because we see ourselves as separate from God.

I invite you to consider, perhaps more abundantly than you may have, our entirely natural connection with God, our ultimate nonseparability. Such a view helps relinquish helplessness and fear—you're not a mere chunk of matter, but an indestructible being.

I've immensely enjoyed writing this book, chapter by chapter, but in finishing it, I faced my biggest challenge. Cruising through, line-by-line, making sure my meaning is clear and the text is free of contradictions, I found it impossible to make my arguments airtight.

My realization: Any point could be contested, should the reader desire. Blessedly, I came across a saying by the great Eastern philosopher, Lao Tzu: *Eternal truths cannot be told in what men write or say.* Language is inherently imperfect.

I believe in God, but not as one thing, not as an old man in the sky. I believe that what people call God is something in all of us. I believe that what Jesus and Mohammed and Buddha and all the rest said was right. It's just that the translations have gone wrong.

— John Lennon

Consider this: Eternal truths are about the unity of everything, about connection, and about the nonseparability quantum physics addresses. The language we use is based on the feedback we get from our senses that present us with illusory pictures of reality. The words we use to explain reality, to explain infinity or God, are always insufficient. Our attempts to *speak* truth—or write it—are forever inadequate. Truth, just like Love, must be experienced.

CHAPTER 21

All Your Prayers Answered? Here's How...

Since childhood, I prayed off and on: *God, please, fix my legs!* For years, nothing happened. Until... I changed the way in which I prayed. Could there be right and wrong ways to pray?

Pray for me! How many times have we said these words? It's a deep seated-belief — even among those who wouldn't publicly identify themselves as adherents of any particular faith — that prayer *works*. A Duke Medical Center clinical trial sought to investigate this belief.

The project bore the name MANTRA II (Monitoring and Actualization of Noetic Training). MANTRA II was the first large-scale study where rigorous scientific protocols were applied, to evaluate the effectiveness of intercessory prayer, the act of praying to God of behalf of others.

For three years, 748 cardiology patients were involved. Twelve prayer groups were solicited from major world religions to pray systematically for 748 cardiology patients in all, throughout the period of three years.

The results, released in 2005, shocked the public. Statistically: null results. No correlation between prayer and medical consequences. The Duke study confirmed the verdict of an earlier Mayo Clinic study of 799 patients: Getting someone to pray for you just doesn't work.

Something was not right. So in 2006 Harvard professor Herbert Benson decided to conduct another experiment: Study of the Therapeutic Effects of Intercessory Prayer (STEP). It was the largest prayer study so far, also called the Great Prayer Experiment. A group of Roman Catholic monks and members of three other Christian denominations prayed for the patients. They were "allowed to pray in their own manner, but they were instructed to include the following phrase in their prayers... *for a successful surgery with a quick, healthy recovery, and no complications.*"

Results: The prayed-for patients showed, overall, no significant improvement. Still worse, major complications and thirty-day mortality occurred in 52 percent of those who received prayer, compared to 51 percent of those who receive none.

Anyone who believes in the power of prayer has to ask: What went wrong? Could these results be real?

So many prayers, you'll note, are petitions. Prayers that beg. Prayers that plead. Yet the most successful and happiest people you meet get very much of what they want, all without the endless *asking*. Why? Because there are the universal laws that must be followed, even in prayer.

Asking, praying for anything is something we do only from a feeling of lack, out of discontent from what *is*. Unless those desires are fulfilled, we'll suffer to some degree or another. Until then, we live in the clutches of our wishes, in fear that our desires might never be satisfied. We feel *inadequate*. And we can never bring abundance into our life from a place of inadequacy.

Acknowledging the good that you already have in your life is the foundation for all abundance.

— Eckhart Tolle, *A New Earth: Awakening to Your Life's Purpose*

Think about this: We don't pray to God for what we already have in abundance. Do you pray for air? For water, when you live on a lake? We pray only for what we feel is in short supply. We ask for what we think is *limited*.

For example, you want a high-paying job. And you know there's a limited supply of those—especially in tight times. You know everyone else is praying for the same thing. And you know everyone else is just as important to God as you are. So you start to settle for less.

You not only wait but also *expect* to wait. You're settling, waiting "your turn." You "know" that maybe it's "not meant to be" that you'll get this job. *Better luck next time,* you say to yourself—setting yourself up for failure, excusing and justifying failure on that contrived ground. Subconsciously, you don't really expect what you're praying for to come right away. And it doesn't.

The physical world is a domain of opposites. However,

the Higher Power, which Jesus calls Love, has no opposites, knows no opposites. Love, remember, "does not insist on its own way." Love responds to our state of mind. It will match exactly what we're vibrating.

Love doesn't know negatives, *No* and *Do not*... Love only agrees with what you're vibrating. It matches your feelings, not so much your words. When you pray, *I don't want to get sick*, and feel desperate, it reads your emotion: I *do want to get sick* and gives you more of the same.

Instead, focus on the thought, *I'm feeling healthy in my (name any organ or body part)*. This phrase, repeated several times, relaxes your facial muscles and sends joyful impulses through your body. That energetic wave is capable of building renewed health.

We often get what we *don't* want, because we expend more energy focusing on the negatives that *might* happen, instead of focusing on what we really *want* to happen. As a result, we bring about what we fear most.

I even heard an acquaintance of mine scolding his mother in a fit of anger: "Don't pray for me because when you ask for something not to happen, it happens."

The real question is not that oldie-goldie: *Why do bad things happen to good people?* The question to ask is: *Why do good people have bad thoughts?* Why do they concentrate on fear, anxiety, or on their smallness?

Think about the last time you were in a bad mood and showed it. How did others respond? Did you feel some were particularly negative toward you? If they were, perhaps it wasn't their fault, but rather a result of the emotion they were instinctively reading in your own energy.

We've all seen it in daily life, many times, and it's one of the strongest sociological forms of evidence for the law of attraction. All of us have had to endure people who made us feel down, angry, resentful, or depressed the second we saw them. They didn't have to say a word. All it took was one look at their negative demeanor, and we felt similar emotions rise in us.

Others we know are quite the opposite — people who, as the clichéd but true expression goes, "light up the room." They always seem friendly and fun. They make you smile. See them, and your day brightens right away.

It's true for an individual, for a group of people, and also demonstrates the law in operation in the whole universe: Like attracts like.

Most of us have a sense of prayer that's all about *asking*. Endless, endless petitions… Give me this! Let me have that! When all your prayers are petitions, you'll never be satisfied.

When you're sick, you ask God to give you health. Then when you're healthy, you'll ask to repair your marriage. Then for your kid to be accepted by that great private school … on and on it goes. So much of what we want is physical. Yet nothing material gives us lasting happiness. We're good for a day, then… *Gimme*.

If we beg for something in a prayer, we've placed ourselves in the state of lacking that very thing, and we get more of the same — it thus feels that our prayer hasn't been answered. If we concentrate on a lack or limitation, we'll achieve only one thing: We'll live in a perpetual state of unhappiness.

Whether you're praying for yourself or for someone else,

don't pray from desperation, from a fever of worry, fret, and doubt. The law of attraction always applies to bring back what you're sending out. Prayer soaked in anguish and doubt can hardly be expected to return brightly positive results.

Truth be known, we don't need to *ask* for anything. We need to shift our focus, and be grateful for what we already have.

Decide to be grateful! Keep it up, and you'll never run out of reasons for gratitude. At any moment, in any situation, however worrisome, there's an endless list of factors for which to be grateful. Seeing and delighting in that list takes a shift in attitude. Focus first not on the things you lack or want, but on the treasures you already have. The foremost of these: life itself.

Asking God for something, and especially when begging or demanding, means you are not fully content. Your gratitude is *conditional*. This won't do. You can't attract what you want into your life by *needing* it. Only from a state of gratitude — as if you already had it — will you acquire it.

Pray prayers of gratitude. Just… *Thanks*. No, I'm not saying simply to *begin* your prayer with thanks — that's common enough advice. If you did list all the things you had to be grateful for, you'd never have time to ask for anything. I'm saying: pray prayers of *nothing* but thanks. Whatever your circumstance, you'll feel better. It's impossible *not* to feel good when you're grateful.

Think of several people you're grateful for in your life. Half a dozen at least. Think of those who've helped you — someone who was there for you when you needed it… people who influenced your life… a person who gave you a life-changing idea.

You can express your gratitude in a phone call. Write a note of thanks and mail it. (Nobody does that anymore, which will make the gesture a powerful one for your card's recipient.) But such overt expressions really aren't necessary. What is important is that you express your gratitude in your heart. *Feel* it.

The recipient of your gratitude most likely will get a warm feeling — a few minutes, perhaps a few hours. But it is *you* who will be the main beneficiary of your expressed gratitude.

Being in a state of gratitude is the most receptive state for inviting good things into your life. The more grateful you are, the better.

Now think of the people who've done something "bad" to you. (I know there is a list!) When Nick decided to marry me, his father took him to visit every relative within a 50 mile radius, so each would convince a would-be bridegroom not to marry a girl with a disability. They acted from their best intentions and in his best interests, but it hurt me nevertheless.

Recently, as I reflected on this event, I became overwhelmed with gratitude toward Nick's relatives. Their words provided impetus for me to work on my legs to make them "normal." Now I see it clearly: I *needed* this experience.

Nothing less traumatic would have been enough to get me out of my feeling-sorry-for-myself state. I haven't actually called them and expressed this gratitude, because they might not understand. But I am sending them love nevertheless, because I'm genuinely grateful.

If you think back on your life's unpleasant episodes and the people who've hurt you, you'll see it wasn't bad at all. You *learned* something and you are better off (not necessarily in a material sense), as a result. You had to learn a lesson and they taught you. Don't they deserve your gratitude? (Eye rolling is totally acceptable here!)

Express gratitude to *everyone* who's made a difference in your life. Being in a state of gratitude is the best way to see solutions to life's problems. Be grateful—as if the solution is already there. Remember Mark 11:24: "Therefore I tell you, whatever you ask for in prayer, believe that you have received it, and it will be yours." Pray as if you already *have it*, that is in gratitude.

Prayers *do* get answered, but not when those prayers come from a position of powerlessness, worthlessness, and wretchedness. Prayers get answered when you're in a state of assurance that everything you could ever want or need is already yours, and being deeply grateful for that grace.

CHAPTER 22

Secret Wisdom From the Past

When my husband and I immigrated to America, we were lovingly welcomed into a Church of Christ, and I became a Christian. I remember hearing the story from John 9 for the first time... Jesus sees a man who's been blind since birth. His disciples ask: Why was this man born blind? Who sinned — he or his parents? "Neither," says Jesus. Rather, this happened so that "the works of God might be displayed in him."

The explanation of that passage went as the following: An afflicted person should embrace a life of suffering for God's purpose and glory. For me, who likewise felt singled out for a disability, this interpretation of Jesus' words felt totally unsatisfying. There *had* to be another explanation, a deeper meaning, less obvious than what lays on the surface. Interestingly enough, it was quantum mechanics that helped me to see that deeper meaning.

Many people believe that Jesus taught in parables so that

his message would be clear — understandable to all. Some Biblical scholars believe otherwise. Even Jesus' disciples did not fully grasp what He meant and often asked Him to explain: "Why do you speak unto them in parables?" He answered, "Because it is given unto *you* to know the mysteries of the kingdom of heaven, but unto them it is not given." (Matthew 13:10-11).

The purer, more powerful a truth, the less likely that "everyone" will know it.

Every religion harbors secret wisdom, largely withheld from the masses. Often, that wisdom hides itself in plain view, yet never is seen by most. This "secret religion" of the elite exists side by side with the more accessible common religion of ordinary believers.

We find such "secret" knowledge everywhere among ancient peoples. The mysteries were guarded with jealous zeal by spiritual masters against all outsiders, and revealed only to the most earnest and worthy disciples. There was no greater crime than the betrayal of these secrets to the uninitiated.

What, exactly, was concealed? Good question. It was in part the same understanding that quantum mechanics reveals to those who possess the courage to make a leap into the unknown.

Quantum mechanics implications unquestionably refute the separability principle that classical physics took for granted. Everything in the universe is manifested from the quantum field by the attention we give it. There is no reality independent of you or me, any more than there is a performance without an audience.

We all hold different notions of God (whether by that or any other name). Whatever your vision of God may be, surely it encompasses the entire universe, and all the laws by which it operates. One of the most astounding of these laws is: *What you have believed will be done for you* (Matthew 9:29).

The woman on the bus in the angel story, the one we met in Chapter 6, believed her life was dreary… painful… unfair. She didn't see a way out, so she believed no way out existed. Not surprisingly, she kept getting what she believed in — endless "crap." *What you have believed will be done for you.*

An opposite scenario… You see no solution to your challenge, perhaps, at this moment, but you *believe* one exists. You believe, moreover, that the very *best* outcome for you is headed your way. And… it happens! Once again: *What you have believed will be done for you.*

Doesn't this sound a lot like the law of attraction? It wasn't a New Age concept after all!

We've been hearing that *Ya gotta* BELIEVE message for ages, but it needs some clarification. *What you have believed will be done for you* is a universal law. Whether you've believed in the best, the worst, or something in between — that's what's coming for you. The law is about belief, but doesn't require your belief in the law itself. This law is in force. Working. Always. Just as the law of gravity.

Matthew 9:29 comes to us in many translations. Here's another one: *According to your faith, be it done unto you.* As you can see, the words *faith* and *belief* are used interchangeably, but they're not the same.

What's the difference between faith and belief? Faith *includes* belief. You definitely must believe that something exists in order to have faith in it. To have faith in someone is putting trust in him.

The term *faith* is always associated with *positive* outcomes: healings, blessings, miracles — anything good that happens beyond what we could imagine. These results accrue when there is trust in a loving Higher Power, regardless of the name we give it.

The verse, *According to your faith be it done unto you,* relates to those cases when you put your trust — fully, deeply — in a power infinitely greater than yours, and you *know for sure* the solution is coming, just as you know the sun will come up tomorrow.

Have you ever wondered why Christ would need *our* faith in Him? Quantum physics implications suggest an entirely different possibility. He wanted us to have faith, to use quantum physics terminology, in *nonseparability* between us and God. He wanted us to believe that, when we realize our unity, our connectedness, with God, we can move mountains. The faith Jesus wants us to have is: *God is Love.*

And the stronger your faith that God is Love, the lesser your self-defeating beliefs can take root.

That is how I see it. First, a simple thought comes to mind: *I want to meet a perfect partner.* And because you have faith that God *is* Love, your belief kicks in: *I'll be spending the rest of my days with my true soulmate.* You *know* that person is on his or her way to meet you, just as you know that the day follows night. With that kind of belief, rooted in that kind of faith, there's no limit to *your* creative power — no limit, that is, to your capacity to manifest your desires.

We do not have even a morsel of faith to move mountains. It's not that we'll be punished post mortem for our lack of faith. We are already punishing ourselves, living a life tormented by conflicts and not realizing we have the power to solve all our problems. Seeing ourselves separate from the source, the Father, is the error we need to correct.

The message of Christ is not about enduring your miserable lot. It's not about tolerating a disability, or any other adversity. Rather, it's about exercising your faith and transcending that problem of yours.

I believe Jesus also meant this: People placed in extremely difficult situations are there for a reason—so that dire necessity can drive them to realizing their oneness with God, and to triumph over their challenges. So if your problems are big… Good. You might thereby have an easier time to move your mountain, so that "the works of God may be displayed" in you.

I'm sure some of you reading this book will write to me asking: "Are you a Christian?" I used to think I was—in a simple, straightforward way—until I gave it more thought: What *is* a Christian, anyway?

The most common answer: someone who believes in Christ. But that couldn't be right—not at face value. "Even the demons believe—and shudder." And demons couldn't be called Christians.

So a more accurate definition might be: someone who does as Christ did. Well, what did Christ do? He became—or, for some other theologies, was—one with God. According to this definition, it's hard to find *anyone* who qualifies as a true Christian, who has "faith to move mountains," who does "even greater things than" Christ. So yes, it's my greatest desire to realize that God and I are inseparable, and by that elevated definition, to become a Christian.

In John 14:13 Jesus says: "Whatever you ask in My name, that will I do..." *Whatever* is an all-encompassing word, but how could this be? No restrictions? Really, none!

In My name means: in the name of Christ. Jesus realized His divine nature. This creative divine power, quantum theory hints, is a power we all have.

Have faith that God *is* Love. Have faith that God and you are inseparable. Be aware of the divine law *What you have believed will be done for you*, and you can make your own distinctive "whatever" come into your life. But only if you have that faith... do you have that power.

CHAPTER 23

Do Not Judge —You Can't Afford It!

In my twenties, whenever I saw girls wearing short skirts, I passed unkind judgment on them. I thought they were just downright *immoral*, and, to my chagrin, sometimes I even voiced my harsh opinion. (The men I knew didn't seem to be bothered by this fashion phenomenon. Go figure!)

But here's the real story… In those days, *I* had no choice but to wear long skirts or pants, trying to hide a two-inch difference in the length of my legs. No Carnaby Street micro-mini for me.

Now, let's fast-forward my life to age 42. I had surgery to lengthen my shorter leg. And guess what? Other women's skirts stopped bothering me, no matter how short. Now, *I* wanted to wear miniskirts myself! Nothing like a little perspective.

My judging had been just a projection of my jealousy. These days, when I encounter a woman griping about, or frowning upon, someone else's belly button ring… a short top…

a bit too much cleavage… or something glitzy, like a pair of metallic leggings or vinyl jeans, I feel a pinch of compassion. She reacts this way mainly because *she* can't wear those things.

It's true of her, of me, of all of us: Our criticism of others discloses more about us than about them. In lamenting others' shortcomings, we broadcast our own unfulfilled desires, insecurities, frustrations, and fears. Why would we bother to comment on someone else, unless our criticism corresponded to something inside us?

Recently, we had a visit from a longtime friend, Ivan—a nice guy. We were all watching a famous male singer performing with a group of beautiful, remarkably long-legged young women. Ivan pointed at the singer and surprised us by saying, "Must be in his late sixties, yet he's always with these young girls."

"You're jealous, Ivan, aren't you?" I meant it as joke. Although a moment later, I regretted my thoughtless remark, as his face betrayed an admission. He seemed equally flustered by his own reaction. Turns out, Ivan had long harbored the desire to be a professional singer, but thought he'd grown too old.

Once you understand how criticism works, and grasp its reflective nature, two things begin to happen. First, the criticism you hear about yourself no longer stings. Second, you'll begin feeling compassion for your critics. Through their words, you'll see the drama that's being played out in *their* lives.

I recall one of my subscribers—I'll call him Fred—who unsubscribed from my e-newsletter. His reason was that he took offense at my occasionally eating raw eggs. *Your chicken-fetus eating for B12 has grossed me out. I've lost all confidence in you.*

One of the most barbaric things in this world is women who eat animals. Goodbye.

I do know that feeling. It only looks like Fred is tough with me for eating an occasional raw egg, or with millions of other women who eat meat. In reality, he's being tough on himself. One suspects there's something in Fred's life, something within him, that he deeply wants to change, much more than my way of getting B12 into my raw food diet.

Not only that, his resentment fuels the very issue he wants to change. If you want to avoid cruelty to animals, harboring negative feelings toward people who eat meat doesn't help. Whatever we object to emotionally, we make stronger. What happens whenever a book or a movie gets negative press? Sales go through the roof.

Just by resenting it, you're contributing to and, in a way, supporting the issue. Instead, focus on the fact that millions are improving their health by choosing to eat more fresh organic garden foods.

Happily, organic food sales have increased *thirty* times in the USA since 2000. By accentuating the positive, you'll be making the world healthier and more humane. (I know — sweep in front of my own door. You're right. *I* need to make fewer presumptions myself. And watch my language, while I'm at it.)

Every time *I* criticize someone, I'm at least implicitly placing myself on a higher plane than the person I'm censuring. And when you're on that higher plane, how do you see someone? — By looking down on him or her.

When I don't like a book or some other creative work and feel strong negative emotions arising in me, I ask myself: *What is it within me that resonates with this work? Do I envy that person's success? Does the work present some kind of accomplishment I believe I can't ever match? Does it make me uncomfortable because it tells me something I need to know, but don't want to hear?*

Sometimes such a work lacks quality, in my perception, and I'm looking from lofty heights as if *I'm* the expert, needing neither learning nor improvement. Here's what I tell myself in such cases: That work in front of me, is my chance to exercise love, compassion, and tolerance. Somebody cared enough, to give up a considerable part of his life to create that work — an achievement that in itself merits praise. Plus, it teaches me how *not* to do things.

This brings us to the issue of "constructive criticism." When asked to critique somebody's work, or when volunteering to do so, what counts as truly constructive criticism? One vital element defines constructive criticism: does it encourage and stimulate the recipient to grow and use your advice as stepping-stones, and not give up on the project altogether?

Aside from constructive criticism, rarely do we criticize for someone *else's* good. Even though that's our apparent intention, too many times (and often too late), I've realized my real motivation. Usually, it's one or both of these: making myself feel good, or making myself look better compared to the person I've judged. What did I get from judging? No more than a moment of moral superiority. That feeling rapidly disappears and leaves a bad aftertaste.

Unless you're in the business of giving advice, unless you're paid to improve somebody's performance, unless you're invited, you're better off not criticizing. When we busy ourselves scrutinizing others' flaws, harboring resentment toward people different from us, we damage ourselves. Resentment, a wise man once said, is a unique fluid: It corrodes only the vessel that contains it.

If it's not for the other person's sake that you'd want to hold back your criticism, do it for your own sake. You get back what you send out. Remember: The closer we are to the state of love, the more creative power we have. We must avoid unkind criticism at all costs. To find genuine happiness in life, we cannot afford negative thoughts—especially those that may lead to strong, continuing negative emotions.

"Stop judging others." Yeah, we've heard that before. The trouble is: Any attempt to stop judging others is doomed to failure so long as we believe the "others" we're judging are separate from us.

Ancient wisdom teaches that not a single ray of light would judge another, for all know their common Source.

When we catch ourselves criticizing or judging others, it's helpful to remember the principle of quantum nonseparability. All is energy. If I emanate harmful emotions, thereby attracting more of the same, I'll be the one who will be hurt.

"Don't judge others because they sin differently from you." This is just a saying, but its profundity strikes me. The word *sin*, translated from Greek and Hebrew, originates in archery and literally refers to missing the "gold" at the center of a target. We all have sinned by giving into the illusion that we're separate from God, and as a result, we all "fall short of the glory of God." In other words, we "miss the target."

Each of us suffers the "disease of ignorance," thanks to our senses' illusionary and deceptive nature. In India, people act compassionately toward prisoners. Their attitude: *We're all criminals — they're the ones who got caught.* Even in a common thief, they'll see a poor soul that merely forgot its divine nature.

If we were honest with ourselves, and self-aware, we'd see we're not capable of a rightful judgment. To judge someone rightly, you'd have to know that person through every moment of their life, their thoughts, emotions, interactions with others — *everything*, else the judgment would be amiss.

If her past were your past, her pain your pain, her level of consciousness, your level of consciousness, you would think and act exactly as she does.

— Eckhart Tolle

Experience shapes each of us uniquely. True non-judging sees any condition, any act, or any person as being in its rightful place for learning purposes. I keep reminding myself: Who am *I* to deprive another of his right to develop his soul with whatever experience he chooses?

On occasions, when I've managed to sustain prolonged moments of non-judgmental attitude to life, I realize that having a judging outlook is energy draining for body and mind. An accepting and loving attitude toward others, in contrast, will energize you, revitalize you, and facilitate your own growth.

Our journey toward experiencing Infinite Love has to start with the surrender of judgment. Only when seeing God in all things: giving each person, each thing, each situation its right to exist, do we begin to vibrate at those frequencies where God can be "found."

CHAPTER 24

Creating Harmony in Your Relationships

When we're in a *deeply* dreadful relationship, the decision to leave may come easily. It's when the relationship is so-so, half-good and half-bad, that we feel truly stuck.

We're not happy. Still, there's just enough good that we can't bring ourselves to quit. Perhaps we feel an obligation, or a need for security. We're afraid to disappoint, or be disappointed, afraid of failure. So we're torn. Result: We concentrate on what we *don't* like in our partner, and that only intensifies our misery. That misery becomes "his fault"... "her fault"... and the cycle perpetuates itself.

A trying relationship can happen anywhere — marriage, family, or the workplace. If you can't just leave, what *can* you do?

Hating the situation you're in won't change it. To hate, to constantly design ways to retaliate for offense, to weigh your losses, to make another endure the same suffering he brought you... all these emotions cost you dearly. They pull negativity toward you. All that ultimately hopeless wheel spinning will only bring you more of the same old negative feelings and make you *resonate* with full-blown hate, desperation, and misery.

We so often say to ourselves: *If this or that happens, then I'll be happy.* In reality, it's the other way around. Your past emotions are the source of the circumstances you're experiencing now.

Since your thoughts powerfully influence your emotions, to start *feeling* better, you need to harbor more positive, more uplifting thoughts.

Emotion, like everything else, is energy. Emotions are indicators of how your beliefs are playing out in your life. Emotions are your friends. They tell you which thoughts are good... and which are destructive.

When you "can't" withdraw from an unhappy relationship, it's time to change. But change what? Trying to change that other person will not work. I've tried that many times. I'll wager that you have, too.

One clear, certain answer: *Change what you focus on* in that other person. Remind yourself that everyone has a good side and concentrate there. Second, do acknowledge what you don't like. *Acknowledge,* I said—not dwell on. Then, negate that negative, and act as if it has already changed.

The emotional frequency you radiate is what you'll attract as real-life experiences or circumstances. Whatever you want in life, begin by acting as if it's already here, present in your life. *Feel* your desired energetic blueprint, and *then* it will materialize.

I remember the day when it dawned on me that the only person I could change in the relationship was myself. It has become a turning point in our marriage. We were sitting in church then, and when it came time for prayer, I took my husband's hand and held it, stroking it gently throughout. From that day on, when he was being "difficult," I remained loving and soft spoken, a big contrast to my previous defensive responses, which had always escalated into arguments.

Nick was a macho man. At first, even though he was bewildered by the change in me, he stood his ground. But soon things between us began to improve. My changed attitude changed my behavior, and, as a result, he had no choice but to change as well.

You cannot cultivate love in yourself for long and not have an effect on others around you. The next five years of our marriage were pretty good, and the last fifteen have been the best ever.

Do not beg, nag, or cajole another person to change. Make a change in your own behavior, and this will create a situation in which the other person will have to respond differently.

Do the opposite of whatever you've been doing. For example, if you've often complained that your spouse is not doing this or that, start praising him at every opportunity, just for the heck of it. Look hard, if you have to, for something to praise. If you can't praise the meal, praise the sauce, praise the neat place settings, but praise *something!*

Suppose you've been the typical "responsible parent," solid as a rock. Yet your teen is threatening to run away. Refuses to do this, insists on doing that. You become more and more stern. Instead, go the other way. Show some affection. Smile when he least expects it. Listen. When your son comes home with a hairstyle you resent, get a wild hairdo yourself, and say you hope his friends will approve. Stop being predictable! Do what you've never done before. Surprise them! Catch your kid or spouse off guard.

You get the idea. It's not possible to give advice for each particular case, and it's not necessary. Once you change your point of view, you'll come up with even better options to improve the difficult relationships in your life.

Why, you may ask, does something in that person make me *squirm*?

Through honestly analyzing what you don't like about that person, you can learn a great deal about yourself. Treat that other person's beliefs, opinions, attitudes, and actions as signs that point to flaws in your own personality, flaws on which you need to work.

A power struggle collapses when you withdraw your energy from it. Power struggles become uninteresting to you when you change your intention from winning to learning about yourself.

— Gary Zukav

He's there so you can see *your* weaknesses, which will facilitate a change in yourself. Plan on learning patience. Count on having to swallow some pride and eat some crow. Figure on becoming more assertive, or learning to formulate your needs more clearly. The solution lies in your personal growth, whether physical, emotional, or spiritual.

In the end, you'll agree: That other person, the one you'd earlier thought of as *difficult*, now deserves your gratitude for making you stronger and wiser.

Express that gratitude—not necessarily in words—and you'll see either of two things happening: Either that person will change... or will no longer be part of your life because he or she is no longer a match for the vibration frequency you emanate.

One common belief stands at the root of all relationship problems: our believing that others should make us happy.

Our son married at age 33. Kind of late, as far as our extended family is concerned. Most married in their early twenties. So, for the past decade, our relatives have expressed their crushing disappointment to my husband Nick and me. *Oh, you poor dears—you don't have grandchildren. So sad, we can't imagine life without them. They bring us happiness...*

I imagine it would be wonderful have grandkids one day. Still, I'm convinced that you cannot *live for* another person. Not for your spouse. Not for your children or grandchildren. If you do, if you try, your very core becomes unstable—you are totally dependent on the actions of *others* to make you happy.

The reason for "the empty nest syndrome" and its attendant loneliness is that we've come to expect happiness to be supplied by others—by a spouse, children, grandchildren, or friends. What an enormous demand that is: *Make me happy!* It's too much to ask from anyone.

The reason we don't have problems with complete strangers is that we don't expect love and security from them.

The precious things you cannot buy, like love and security, can only come from within. It's a state you create inside yourself, which cannot be handed to you by the outside world, nor by your immediate family.

The only power, the only immediate power you have is the power over your thoughts. That power over your own thoughts is *all* you need to lead the life you want. Remember, you cannot have a negative emotion when you're holding on to a positive thought.

Put feeling good *first!* Good things will follow. You must *feel* better before your life will *become* better. You must smile before others smile back at you.

You *can* change a troubled relationship. You've been creating it all along. It's now just a matter of adjusting it to the way you want it to be.

CHAPTER 25

Intuition and Ego: Who's Talking?

Some time ago, I was talking to a yoga instructor who was quite unsympathetic about my hip limitations. I told him that his words hurt my feelings.

I'll never forget what he said: *No one can hurt your feelings unless you have a wound that his or her words can rub. Heal your psychological wounds, and the words of others can never hurt you. Would you be hurt if someone said you have purple hair (assuming you don't)? No, you'd think it's silly or funny, but you'd never feel hurt.*

The truth of his lesson hit me like a brick. I haven't been the same since. Moreover, I began noticing when and how my ego talks. Not all the time, but at least when it's at its loudest.

Words carry precisely the meanings we give them. Our reactions to someone's words can tell stories about *us*.

Suppose someone announces: *You will NEVER get married.* If you were married, this comment would simply seem odd, misplaced. It might raise an eyebrow, but it wouldn't stir any anger or resentment in you. But, what if you're single and hoping to marry someday? Imagine, too, that the clock's ticking, and perhaps you've been unlucky in love. Now the comment would feel hurtful indeed. Why? Because it's *your* ego, that holds doubts and worries about you getting married.

You hurt my feelings... We've all heard that line endless times. Is there anyone alive who hasn't said it? But consider: Nobody can hurt your feelings without your consent.

Example... Your daughter's angry. She tells you: *You're a lousy mother!* The extent to which this remark hurts you depends on the degree you *allow*. Whether your behavioral response is a flood of saddened tears or a nasty barb tossed back, some part of you believes it's true.

If you didn't buy into it, then you'd perhaps just calmly ask your daughter to "unpack" what she means. Or you might just ignore her remark. If you're truly not owning the notion that you're a "lousy mother," you wouldn't act, you wouldn't feel offended, and you wouldn't respond defensively.

What angers us in another person is more often than not an unhealed aspect of ourselves. If we had already resolved that particular issue, we would not be irritated by its reflection back to us.

— Simon Peter Fuller

The words of others hold *only* the meaning *we* give them. The meaning is, quite literally, in your head. The source of our problems is that we believe in our own versions of ourselves.

That's ego! We believe the stories our ego tells on our behalf. Sure, there are facts. But what we make of them, how we interpret them, is fiction. The ego loves bringing drama into our lives.

Every ego builds its own universe, and parks itself at the center. For example, my ego tells me I'm important. Indeed, I'm just about *the* most important person my ego knows. If I didn't believe my ideas were clever and original, would I get defensive if someone challenged them? If I didn't believe I deserved to be praised for my achievements, would I feel hurt if someone criticized me? The problem is never with others. It's always with *me ... us.*

If your ego's busy pretending it's the hub of the galaxy, it may be time to stop guarding your self-image. It's also time to be more conscious of the ego's power, of its having its hand in *everything*. Every word I say here is directed to myself, in the first instance.

Who owes you? Owes you what? Money? Service? Respect? Special consideration? If you believe others owe you blessings, you'll always sense the whiff of threat in the air, amid the reek of disappointment. Who'll be next to tick you off? Did someone shortchange you? Not show up on time? Who'll get something—a stock deal, a smart phone, a sandwich—you didn't get?

The ego's greatest fear is its own death. It's fanatical about survival. It's an expert on how to adapt to external conditions. The ego is there to assure our survival in the material world. It's good we're programmed to listen to our ego in critical situations, such as when we need to run for our lives.

The challenge is not to let your ego take over your life, not to let it become the entirety of who you are.

The ego is seriously shortsighted. It's totally under the influence of our senses. Ego *believes* those senses — utterly. Your ego wants you to believe you are *separate* from others and from God. Your ego wants you to feel "better" than others. That's the only way an ego can feel important, and you're only "better" if you're *other*.

We might think, then, that having a *small* ego is a way to freedom. Really, both extremes are pathological — the tiny ego and the enormous one. Both are products of insecurity and of ignorance about our true nature. To feel bigger than or lesser than others is always symptomatic of a sick ego.

The big ego constantly compares itself with others, defines itself in terms of others — and falls short. Because it can never be better than everyone else, the owner of that ego can never be happy.

The small ego, likewise, defines itself in terms of others. The smaller-ego person holds a lower opinion of herself, ignorant about her own significant role in this world. She never lives up to her full potential and feels perpetually unhappy. It's important that we keep our egos healthy. Not too big, not too small.

In making challenging decisions, we need to listen to another voice within us. That voice is intuition. Some believe it is the voice of our soul, or the voice of our Higher Self. Notice you get intuitive prompts from your soul all the time. Trust your intuition, that curious ability to understand something instantly, without the need for deliberate conscious reasoning.

One definition of happiness: feeling that you are where you should be. Whatever you do, whatever you plan to do, must *feel right*.

How can you learn to discern whether you're listening to your *ego*, or to your *intuition*? It isn't always easy, but there are ways to tell.

The ego *thinks*... the intuition *feels*. In thinking, you can hear the wheels turning. Intuition... well, it just *knows*.

Ego—the mind, if you will—reasons its way to conclusions. Intuition, on the other hand, is a means of directly perceiving truth or fact, independently of any indirect reasoning process. And, yes, intuition often conveys ideas that are not, or do not seem, rational.

The intuitive mind is a sacred gift, and the rational mind is a faithful servant. We have created a society that honors the servant and has forgotten the gift.

— Albert Einstein

The ego is most often past-oriented. It's all about learning from experience, reasoning from one occasion to the next, recalling how it used to be and expecting that same thing again. The ego plays it safe, plays by the rules. The intuition is daring, risk taking.

The ego seeks to protect your image, your identity, at all costs. It will insist you do what's good for your ego, regardless of how it affects others. The intuition, by contrast, tends to hint at solutions that will benefit everyone involved, and never at the expense of somebody else. It will nudge you to seek a solution within yourself.

Ego is founded in fear. Intuition comes from love. Fear is built on "otherness." It's always about "those" people—ugly, filthy, stupid, cruel, immoral, *other* people. Love, though, happens when the framework is: *I'm like you. You're like me. We're connected. We belong to a greater whole.*

Ego insists. Intuition suggests. The ego talks straight to your face: *Do it!* Or else! The ego is hard-edged, often harsh. *This is the right way. Forget everything else.* The intuition's voice is soft-edged, with a kind of neutrality. *We might try this... What do you think of this idea... Here's a way you might go...*

Could you use a sharper intuition? Think of your pineal gland. As small as the pineal gland is—the size of a rice grain and the shape of a pine cone—it's been known for many centuries in numerous cultures, and holds a place powerfully connected with the notion of "seeing beyond."

In ancient Vedic writings, the pineal gland *is* the "third eye." We see a reflection of this in Hindus' placing the red dot, the *tilak,* on their foreheads, representing the third eye. Buddhists, too, believe in a third eye, and statues of the Buddha often appear with large headgear in the shape of a pine cone.

As for the Christian tradition, it's noteworthy that the pinecone appears on the Pope's staff, and the Vatican exhibits the world's largest pinecone statue.

Lost esoteric Christian traditions, Gnosticism among these, revered the pineal gland. Some even believe that in Matthew 6:22, Jesus refers to pineal gland when he says the eye "is the lamp of the body; so then if your eye is clear, your whole body will be full of light."

Science doesn't offer any support to the notion that the tiny pineal gland *is* literally this "third eye." But science does know, for example, that the pineal gland receives more blood flow, relative to its mass and volume, than any other organ in the body — even more than the rest of the brain. That alone says: *Something* special is going on here.

We know, too, that the pineal gland is more active in children than in most adults. We know it has *something* to do with creativity, insight, intuitive thinking, with the subconscious, with the spiritual side of life. We know that the more active the pineal, the more active are those functions within the mind.

When fed the standard Western cooked-food fare that we find in the canned and frozen food sections of supermarkets, as well as in the meat and the junk food sections, the pineal gland literally calcifies, becomes hard. The pineal's larger neighbor, the brain, becomes obstructed with waste, less and less able to regenerate, to recycle, to cleanse, to make new connections. Yet all this is completely redeemable, even reversible.

When you're eating more raw fruits, vegetables, nuts, and seeds, your body is able to cleanse and detoxify harmful substances. You're eating the very foods that best support the pineal gland, cleansing it, nourishing it, activating it, and restoring it to its highest function.

Some of the most important foods for nourishing the pineal gland are: dark leafy greens such as bok choy, spinach, collards, kale, and sea vegetables. The cleaner you are upstairs, from the tiny pineal to the brain itself, the more intuitive you'll become.

The ability to recognize who is talking, ego or intuition,

will make a big difference in the quality of your life. Beware of your ego. So many of your problems are created there. For sound solutions, heed your intuition.

CHAPTER 26

The World Is Your Mirror

A traveler, walking on his way to an unknown distant town, met an old farmer and asked, "What sort of people live in the next town?" Before answering, the old farmer had his own question to ask: "What were the people like where you come from?" The traveler said: "They were a bad lot: trouble-makers, lazy, the most selfish people in the world. I'm happy to be leaving the scoundrels."

"Is that so?" replied the old farmer. "Well, I'm afraid that you'll find the same sort in the next town.

Later, another stranger, coming from the same direction, asked the same question: "What sort of people live in the next town?"

"What were the people like where you come from?" asked the old farmer once again.

"They were the best people in the world. Hard working, honest, and friendly. I'm sorry to be leaving them."

"Don't be sorry," said the farmer. "You'll find the same

sort in the next town."

I love this story. It illustrates brilliantly that the world is our own reflection.

When we have an encounter with a disagreeable person, that occurrence is a direct response to our own inner state. Expect a scoundrel, and you'll meet a scoundrel... Expect a fine person, and a fine person you'll meet.

You're driving on the Interstate and somebody cuts you off. Your first thought: *What a jerk! He's an idiot!* You get angry. Why? Because you hold the belief that the guy who rips in front of you is a *bad person*. Now, you expect him to do something nasty to *you*.

What happens when you change this belief in a particular way?... Imagine that your "jerk" is frantic to get to the next rest stop, or gas station for you-know-what. Late for his first date with that fabulous girl, who'll cast him aside if he doesn't get there on time? Perhaps he's even driving someone to the hospital. We all understand urgency: *Poor fellow, let's hope you'll make it safely!*

Think about it... at very least, this other person — our jerk, or idiot — provides us with an opportunity to exercise acceptance and compassion toward others.

Still, some will say: You need to teach this guy a lesson. *It'll serve him right.* Some will even say you're wrong if you don't.

Understand that this guy, at this moment has been materialized by you for *you* to learn a lesson. The world, in that moment or any, is performing for you and *you* alone. You're the conductor of the symphony, the producer of the show, and the writer of the script.

Our thoughts create that person out of our own short-comings and needs. Don't like a person you meet? You're participating in creating reality, so realize this: Your perception, your presumption, is what's made him as you see him. What attracts you to a person—or repels you—is something in *you*. The "jerk," or "idiot," *I* meet really reflects the idiot, the jerk, in *me*.

Do I look for faults in men?

Then surely I will find them;

Dishonesty, lust, greed, hatred, and all the rest.

All these come with immense fecundity.

Do I look beyond to the good?

Then what a glorious paragon is man!

Generous, kind, and fair-dealing.

Which of these is the real?

Neither and both. Man reflects just what I seek.

— Franklin Merrell-Wolf, Pathways Through To Space

Have you ever been yelled at, accused of something you believed wasn't your fault? We all have. But have you ever answered a bold verbal attack with kindness? Have you gone out of your way to do something nice for that person—something totally unexpected?

On those occasions, when I've managed to turn the other

cheek — I'm still working on this one — it felt good. And it's often produced amazing results.

Our mind is its own world-builder. Would you like that other person to change his behavior, his attitude? Then change yours!

Instead of lowering yourself to your opponent's level, elevate him or her to the level of compassion. See that person transformed. If someone is angry or upset, read her emotions as a cry for love and attention. She doesn't need to be told her emotions are out of proportion to the situation. Likely, she already knows that and just can't help it. But give her some love ... and all of a sudden she's a changed person.

In some cases, the change is almost immediate: She turns charming, full of apology. In other cases, the transformation is slower, but it's there nonetheless — he becomes more thoughtful, less eager to act out anger or resentment. You can bet he'll show more tolerance in his next encounter with somebody else. Keep going! Make it your *modus operandi!* The lives around you will change for the better, and so will yours.

What you intend for others, you intend for yourself. To criticize someone's way of making money is pushing money away from *yourself.* Now, your next thought might be: *But what if he makes his money in a dishonorable way?*

Once again, it's all about you — not about that other guy. You're not here to criticize or to correct somebody's actions. If you see something or someone you don't like, consider: It's likely *your own energy* has attracted that unfortunate behavior, perhaps even attracted the person himself. Uncomfortable thought? I understand. Still, that is how reality operates.

The "wrong" in the universe is not divisible into independent portions that can be attributed to others (e.g. He's greedy. She's envious.). We're all responsible for it—if not with our actions, then with our negative thoughts. The potential for *every* possible mistake resides within each of us. So forget accusations that a certain action or person is "wrong." The best place to start diminishing wrong is within ourselves.

There's a meaning and there's a lesson in every wrongdoing and misdeed we witness, in every "bad" person we encounter. There's something there that's *meant for us*. It's all there for us to learn one important lesson: If we want to receive love, we must first give love.

One idea fascinates me and I'm putting it into practice in my life. It's the concept of *Ho'oponopono*, the ancient Hawaiian ritual of forgiveness and reconciliation.

I am sorry.

Please forgive me.

Thank you.

I love you.

Who'd think that repeating this simple mantra (and meaning it), could profoundly change our own lives, and the lives of those around us?

When a psychologist at a hospital for mentally ill criminals began looking—with love and forgiveness in his heart—at photos of his patients and repeating those four phrases, it led gradually to their healing, their discharge, and the ultimate closing of the hospital.

That therapist believed that the source of the problem was not with the patients, but with his own erroneous thoughts.

When the error in his thinking was corrected, the problems in the patients began to resolve. That doctor was Ihaleakala Hew Len, Ph.D., the man who, with Joe Vitale, wrote the book entitled *Zero Limits,* all about this beautiful forgiveness process called Ho'oponopono.

The term *Ho'oponopono* can loosely be translated as "to do what's right, to correct a mistake." It is a process of letting go of everything that blocks the Infinite Love within you. You must undergo the process yourself. Your erroneous thoughts *can* be transmuted into thoughts of love.

It may sound like a radical concept to take total responsibility, not only for your own actions but for everybody else's as well, but it only *sounds* radical. Like everything else, it's subject to the universal law of cause and effect. The problem is never *out there*. It's within our own mind. By changing internally, we can effect change outside of us.

This is how we make this world a better place—by changing ourselves. And now, everywhere we go, more and more often we'll meet the best people in the world: hardworking, honest, and friendly, people who can love us, because we loved them first.

CHAPTER 27

Turn the Other Cheek... It's Good for *You*!

Our family's former Memphis home stood at the side of a small lake, with about fifteen other houses around it. I loved our back window view—a constant joy in my daily life.

One day, we took a paddleboat around the lake, and I observed how much the view changed as we paddled past each neighbor's house. The lake had never before looked so spectacular. Even seeing our own house from a different angle was a *wow* experience.

It's the same with our beliefs. Once you start paddling around your figurative lake and experience the perspectives of others, investigating their beliefs, you'll find it much harder to presume your perspective is superior, or somehow more "natural."

What you see from your home, your "temple," is your personal, highly subjective truth, which depends entirely on your experiences and your station in life.

Each person's mind hosts a conglomeration of beliefs

and convictions, jammed together to create what we call "I." We say: *I'm a woman of a certain age, I'm a wife, I'm a mother, I'm of a certain nationality, I'm a student, an accountant.* Any one of these characteristics is entirely fine—as long as we do not identify solely with that one marker.

An identity is a defined viewpoint from which life is experienced. There is, of course, an infinitude of possible viewpoints. When looking at matters from others' perspectives, you'll begin to see that insisting that one set of beliefs and convictions is inherently better than another is not only unwise, it's downright dangerous.

As you're reading this, some conflict will be brewing, or already raging somewhere in the world. These conflicts originate because of religious and/or cultural differences, boundary disputes, or national pride, but they cannot be resolved on the level of those labels. We are not our labels.

People take sides because they want a feeling of identity. We must admit that we *need* enemies and adversaries to feel important. Without them, we'd feel empty. But choosing one side will automatically set us in opposition to the other, creating quarrels, conflicts, and wars.

So many of our personal or private truths are all about details. Differences. When we identify as a nationality, an occupational or personality type, we lean toward stereotype. We run the danger of becoming drones, open to exploitation by others. It's imperative that we expand our minds, that we understand both sides of the conflict or quarrel, but identify with neither.

There could be no argument if at least one person had a glimpse of higher spiritual truth. "It takes two fools to have an argument." The possession of truth brings delight, and the desire for argument disappears.

All problems arise from the erroneous view that one is separate from universal oneness. Change that point of view, and problems vanish. Truth is always truth, and nonsense or false beliefs get exposed easily when you change your point of view. It helps to see any conflict from the viewpoint of an alien.

You guys are both saying the same thing. The only reason you're arguing is because you're using different words.

— S. I. Hayakawa, *Canadian-born American academic and politician of Japanese ancestry*

Nothing expressed in words is absolute truth. Words are derived from the material world, itself an illusion that doesn't exist independently of its observer. Every statement contains its own counter-statement. Arguing in words is largely futile. As is arguing by hurling pots and pans, or bullets and bombs.

An eye for an eye' only ends up making the whole world blind.

— Mahatma Gandhi

We've seen it so many times: In a conflict, both sides pray to God, each asking for help to defeat the other. God, however, cannot be found on the low vibrational frequency of hatred and violence. God is Love. To elicit His help, those in conflict must raise the frequency of their emotional states to the level of love.

Jesus said: Love your neighbor. Everybody knows it, but nobody does it. Why not? Because most don't understand the significance of this command and will reap the considerable consequences. We need to realize that the others, the neighbors, are really *ourselves,* in terms of energy. Love is a subconscious realization of nonseparability, and as such, is a state where there can be no enemies.

When we see how others fuss about all the useless things they'll leave behind after they die, we see kindred souls struggling to find life's meaning, but confused by their senses. Compassion arises in our hearts. This is the beginning of loving your neighbor.

Turning the other cheek *works.* Why? Because *attitude* — a gentle attitude, in particular — is the most potent of weapons. If you fight something directly, it only gets stronger. Energy flows where your attention goes. If you hate something, you make it stronger in a negative way. When you send love, you make it stronger in a loving way. You empower everything to which you give your attention. You get back what you send out.

Turning the other cheek is not about submitting to oppression, but rather about not letting your negative emotions — hate, resentfulness, vengeance — add to an already flagging situation. On the larger societal level, turning the other cheek *can* translate — if well managed — as nonviolent protest, or civil disobedience.

During the 1956 bus boycott in Montgomery, Alabama, a bomb exploded on the porch of Dr. Martin Luther King's house while his wife and infant daughter were inside. They were not injured, but it was Dr. King's message of peace that stopped the vengeful crowd from rioting:

"Jesus still cries out in words that echo across the centuries: 'Love your enemies; bless them that curse you; pray for them that despitefully use you.'" We must meet hate with love, King preached.

Influenced by methods Mahatma Gandhi used in his quest for India's independence, King wrote: "As I delved deeper into the philosophy of Gandhi, my skepticism concerning the power of love gradually diminished, and I came to see for the first time its potency in the area of social reform."

Why *are* we instructed to "turn the other cheek?" It's not just for the good of the other person, it's for *our own good*. Love your neighbor—even if he isn't lovable. What you'll find is this: Real forgiveness and love feel great! And you'll attract more— much more—of the positive energy you've always wanted to surround you.

But how does non-violence help things? For starters, it can help *you*. Respond to someone else's initial assault by lashing out, and you're sure to find yourself in a scuffle, or worse. But, relatively few will kick a man when he's down.

Throw a punch... it invites a punch back. The minds of most people tell them they "have to" fight back. Violence—not just the physical kind, but the verbal and emotional kinds, too— escalates. Between nations or tribes or individuals, an "incident" becomes a clash, becomes a war.

Endless cultures, libraries of religious works, so many spiritual leaders all tell us: It's love that will save the world. We never *quite* seem to listen. But we should.

In my time, I've attended many self-growth and spiritual

seminars, of every hue and stripe. I remember this one…

An Indian woman was giving a testimonial. She'd been kidnapped, she told us, by a vicious man who intended to rape and kill her. She was out of her wits from fear. But then she remembered what her spiritual master had been teaching her and she decided to try something based on those teachings.

She said to the man: *I feel a deep compassion to you.*

This was the last thing the man expected: *Are you crazy, woman? Shouldn't you feel sorry for yourself?*

Look, she said. *When you die, you'll go through the life review, your life will be revisited in the reversed order, from the day you die all the way to your birth. And you'll feel all the pain you intend to give to me. You'll feel every bit of my pain. And you'll feel the pain of everyone you ever hurt — you'll feel their pain too. It's a matter of energy*, she explained, *an energy that we all share. We're all one. So whatever you do to me, you'll be doing to yourself.*

She continued with this sermon for some time. Eventually, he let her go, untouched.

Once you become committed to non-violence and people see this, they'll know who you are. You'll become the strong, quiet one. The one about whom the less violent voices will say: *Listen to her… Hear him out…* Around you, in streets and meetings and social situations, violence will begin to disappear, arguments will taper off, or never begin.

Recently, I listened to an interview with a professional negotiator, whose job is to conduct non-violent negotiations with terrorists. Once, to save several people held hostage by brutal bandits, after all else failed, he had to go into their camp to negotiate on their turf. The terrorists said: *We warned you —*

you're going to die. We just want to know what made you come and negotiate for people you've never even met.

Said the negotiator: *It was my investment.*

Investment? Investment in what?

An investment, he said, *so that one day, one of your children will do the same for my children...*

He lived to tell the story. The hostages were freed.

Many see the numerous conflicts across the world as a sign of a coming apocalypse. *Signs of the end times*, they say. Truth be known, historically, all other times also looked rather like the end times. I'm no end-timer. I hold a more optimistic view.

I believe that by teaching the key notion of nonseparability, we can create a more truthful worldview. When we teach our children that on the most basic level, there is no difference between Mary and Johnny, that we're all part of one swirling energy, and that by hurting another, we're hurting ourselves, there will hope for us to live in peace as good neighbors.

CHAPTER 28

Other People's Problems... Resist the Urge

When I was growing up, my grandmother raised chickens. As a child, the arrival of new chicks thrilled me. One day I wanted to get to a chick while it was still struggling to hatch, to help the "poor thing" come out. Grandma quickly grabbed my hand and slapped it to teach me the lesson never to do it again.

Later, I learned: you should never help a chick when it's breaking its way out of its shell. The chick needs to complete the physiological process of hatching *on its own*. "Helping" by chipping off the eggshell means causing it potential harm, deformation, even death.

We've all been on both ends of all kinds of well-intended help.

Early on in our marriage, my husband Nick embarked on a mission to make me happy. At the time, it was hard for me to walk, "No problem," said Nick. I would not *go* to work at all, and *he* would provide. Training my legs was obviously hard, too. Nick's solution: I should stop going to my swimming classes altogether. If I should get to the point of not being able to walk at all, he said, he could always trundle me around in a wheelchair. Like most women, I wasn't quite happy with my looks. I wanted to use makeup and care for my appearance. No need for that, said Nick. I already had *him*. Why would I want to look good for others?

Like a plant getting too much water, I was wilting away. With his good intentions of helping me by "taking away my problems," he also took away some of *me*. I resented it. I wanted to *solve* my problems by *myself*, and not have someone else permanently shoulder them for me.

Years passed before I clearly understood exactly what was making me unhappy. Years more before we both understood: You can't make another person happy. Happiness doesn't come from outside. And you can't solve another person's problems. (If you could, it wasn't really a problem.) It's the *process* of resolving her own challenges that will make that other person happy. A process only she — not you — can experience directly.

We need to be careful never to give help that can hurt. In her latter years, my grandmother left her house to my mom, and not to her other two daughters. It was a small house, not worth much, but my mother appreciated it and treated my grandmother like the most precious artifact.

She saw to her every need and anticipated her every desire. Whether it was gardening, getting the groceries, cleaning the house or making meals, everything my grandma used to do for herself, my mother started doing for her to show her gratitude.

My mom bent over backwards for grandma, even to the extent of retrieving objects that were just a few feet away. In the end, my grandmother lost all muscle tone and became bedridden. Her meals and toilet needs had to be taken care of in her bed, and she remained there until her death.

Perhaps some degeneration was inevitable. Still, had she remained independent, her decline wouldn't have been so fast, nor so drastic. It's a sad story, but there's a lesson to be learned. It's vital that our sacrifice and loving care don't do more harm than good to a recipient.

What about you? When you offer someone help, are you enabling—in the better sense of that word? Or are you disabling?

When we immigrated to the USA, we were poor. As in: *poor.* My husband found a job as a handyman with a landlord who rented his houses through government programs to people on welfare. Sometimes, I helped Nick as a cleaner.

On one occasion, I was on my hands and knees, cleaning floors to get an apartment ready for inspection. The tenant had just been visited by "a nice lady from church," dispensing a pauper's allowance of food, clothing, and trinkets. When the woman left, the tenant cursed loudly. She couldn't stand these belittling handouts from richer folk. It was, for her, *patronizing.* Such help doesn't strengthen. It *weakens.*

We are accustomed to the idea that helping people is good and unselfish. But, help in the sense of "handouts" is rarely good for the recipient, and almost never unselfish.

Before offering your help, ask yourself why you are doing it. And be brutally honest. Do you feel obligated? Do you give help for leverage? Do you feel a need to be seen as "good?"

Do you crave attention and appreciation? Do you feel responsible for everyone around you? Do you like to play the savior? Do you exaggerate other's problems, so you can avoid resolving your own? Do you have a self-sacrifice complex?

This may sound odd to say to someone (like you, perhaps) who likes to cast himself or herself as a helper, but I'll stand by it nonetheless. To go about helping others and ignoring yourself has often been painted as a heroic stance. It would make sense in a finite universe. But we live in an infinite universe, a universe in which you cannot give enough, or sacrifice enough to make the world a better place.

Good and bad run side by side in our material world. Why is it, then, that one person chooses to see good and stays happy most of the time, while another concentrates on particular problems or vices of the world and carries them on his shoulders?

Why does one person devote her life to fight against poverty, another wrestle with global warming, another assert animal rights, and yet another seeks the preservation of whales, or of an endangered flower species? Why are we disturbed by this particular injustice, and not so much by another?

Nearly all of us are quite selective in our choices, and in our caring. An anti-abortion activist may devote little mental energy to the cause of animals euthanized in kill shelters, and vice versa. The choice usually bears no correlation to the magnitude of a particular wrongdoing's impact on humanity (though we often *think* it does). The choice has everything to do with *you* and with *me*.

This or that particular cause has been highlighted by your consciousness, so that you can heal *your* wounds. A woman, whose child was killed by drunk driving, will join MADD—Mothers Against Drunk Driving. The father of a son killed in a war will join the rally against that war.

Typically, once our inner wound has healed, we'll stop feeling affected by this particular frequency on the great spectrum of evils, and we'll move on to something else.

Only when we change our attitude toward death, and get a broader perspective on the purpose the negative serves in the material world, will we stop fighting "evil" altogether. The physical reality with its polarity is already as good as *you* choose to experience it. Is you glass half empty or half full?

Your help cannot be anything but selfish. After all, the reality you're experiencing is your mind's interpretation of your senses. So help for a good selfish reason! The best reason for helping others is to recognize there is no separability, and by making the other person happy, you make yourself happy. Now, you don't need that other person's gratitude, you're always getting your reward.

Help is often resented, which confuses those who like to help. No matter how much we disguise it, help is always given from a higher level, and always contains this message: *I'll do it for you because you cannot do it for yourself.* We reflect their helplessness back to those we help. As children, we rejected help. As adults, we are no different. It feels much better to do it yourself than to be helped.

People are your mirrors. Likewise, you can serve as a reflection of another person's goodness. Concentrate on the *positive* in their character, their life's situation, even on their problems, but don't join them in their misery.

Be a catalyst for their natural development. Encourage

their evolution through your example. By making them feel better about themselves, you're contributing to their own capacity for self-love.

Self-development is a higher duty than self-sacrifice.

— Elizabeth Cady Stanton

Pursue, first, your own growth, your own bliss. *Then* you'll become an example to inspire others. They'll want to be around you. They'll gravitate toward the positive energy you emanate. There's perhaps nothing better you can do for them.

Real help doesn't even look like help. It usually goes by another word: inspiration. You simply reflect another person's goodness and worth—a goodness and worth she might have overlooked.

Change in life begins with change in thought. One free meal doesn't change much (except, for example, in disastrous situations, where such help can save lives). In many cases, an inspiring idea is more valuable than a handout, to get a person going again so that he won't need more handouts. Familiar thought: *Give a man a fish, you feed him for a day...Teach a man to fish, you feed him for a lifetime.*

What does it mean, then, to *help* someone else? Keep in mind one essential while helping another person: Don't stand in the way of his or her growth. Problems are lessons. Those lessons need to be learned. When helping others, make sure you understand the difference between a chick that got tangled in a net, and one that is simply trying to hatch.

CHAPTER 29

Love Yourself… What Does It Mean?

The second commandment Jesus gave us is: *Love your neighbor as yourself.* But why didn't Jesus ever tell us: *Love your neighbor more than yourself?* For the same reason as the announcement you hear on every flight before takeoff — *In the event of cabin depressurization, secure your own oxygen mask first, and then assist the other person …*

Quantum theory implies that, ultimately, *all* things are connected. All people, too. Even the concept of *self* is to be questioned. To begin, the self is a construct. The boundaries between self and others are themselves constructed, contrived, and ultimately illusory.

Once we realize our own connectedness with others, our perceived boundary between self and others begins to blur. And it's precisely there that we begin to see the potential unity of love-for-self and love-for-others.

The first commandment is to love God. And we've already established that there is no crisp, clean separation between you and God. Consequently, the first commandment comes to look a bit like: *Love yourself.*

Consider these two commandments together. What Jesus is really saying here is that you can't truly love your neighbor if you don't love yourself.

The quantum universe now shows us the connectedness between the two sides of this command: how loving ourselves and loving others are intimately related.

So, let me venture my understanding of spirituality: *to love God in yourself and love God in others.* At least, that's how I understand the two greatest commandments given by Christ Jesus.

Self-love means treating yourself as an equal to others — viewing yourself as different, but not better than others.

While growing up, I knew only one person — Margarita, a singer — whom I'd call self-loving. By my definition, she was a profoundly spiritual person, even though Russia was then a Communist country, and she'd never been to church nor had she read the Bible. She was grateful for every moment of life, able to find good in every person she met. She was always cheerful. I never heard her complain, whine, excuse, or criticize others for their failings.

Some people were saying about her: *Oh, she never helps her daughters financially. Her house is a mess when she's on concert tours. She lets her children call her by her first name. She's an eccentric.*

True, she never sacrificed her life for her husband or her children. She chose her career and led — still leads — a fulfilled life. When one of her children wants to leave a grandchild on her doorstep, and she's leaving for the gym, she'll freely say: You'll have to come later. Yet, her daughters and grandchildren adore her.

Here's another scenario... A man works *very* hard to provide for his family. Neglects his health, his rest, and his peace of mind. Comes home so stressed that his wife and children are walking on eggshells, fearful of his temper. Nobody enjoys his coming home. It goes on like this for years and years. Now he's sick, moody, and keeps reminding everyone of his sacrifices.

Altruism, by definition, is unselfish regard or devotion to the welfare of others. Does it really exist? Do we, *can* we, genuinely sacrifice ourselves for others, having little or no regard for ourselves? For my friend Scott, the answer is a resounding yes. That's what the Bible teaches, Scott reminds us: Giving is more blessed than receiving.

Let me ask: Can you ever be anything but a cheerful giver? If you're living under the illusion of separability, it makes sense that the fruits of good deeds are finite. When you see yourself as separate from others, there's not enough good to go around: that if you give, you'll then have less. Then altruism seems noble.

But when you understand the nonseparability principle, you'll know it's you, the giver, who is the main beneficiary of your own giving. It just feels great to help another person. But what's more, by the law of attraction you'll be attracting more goodness to come into your life.

At the church soup kitchen where you volunteer, let's say, the receiver might get a bowl of soup or some turkey, but *you*, as a giver, will be many times more blessed.

So, is giving selfish? Yes, it is, and there's no reason to be defensive about it. Everything you perceive in your world is about you. All of reality is about you.

No man giveth but with intention of good to himself; because gift is voluntary; and of all voluntary acts the object to every man is his own pleasure.

— Thomas Hobbes, English philosopher

Once we realize how giving and receiving truly work, we'll do more good for others.

Self-love and love for others cannot be neatly separated. Think about it: A person who respects himself is generally respectful of others. A person, who forgives his own imperfections, will not see such imperfections in others. A really happy and content person will do no harm. Only a person who hates himself is capable of harming others.

Self-love *doesn't* mean egotism. Egotism is simply *me, me, me.* Egotism begins in fear and craving. Egotism is the inevitable home for the person who believes life and love are zero-sum games — that there isn't enough to go around, and others shouldn't have it — whatever "it" may be. Because *I* want it, and if *they* have it, *I* can't have it.

Egotists aren't givers. You can't give what you don't have. Real love begins in self-love and then extends outward.

The difference between an egotist and a self-loving individual is analogous to the difference between a whirlpool and a geyser. An egotist is coming from a perceived or felt *lack* of love.

He feels there's not enough love, so he, like a whirlpool, is sucking down everything he can get. By contrast, the person full of genuine self-love has so much love that it spills over, like a geyser — there's more than enough for her, and plenty for others around her.

We've all heard that we should love ourselves, but so many of us believe deep inside that we are not lovable, not really worthy of love. Deep in the subconscious mind, we carry the guilt of endless sins, and believe we're going to be punished for them. That's why we don't think we deserve love. And hence, "loving ourselves" never really works. Why? The same issue: an erroneous belief in separability.

We'll continue to suffer that separation until we come to realize we are ultimately inseparable from God, inseparable from the rest of humanity.

What does it mean to *love yourself*? It begins with accepting yourself and giving your attention to what you *like* in yourself, and to stop focusing on what you don't like. Simpler still: Don't think negative thoughts about yourself.

Do you remember when you were falling in love? Research shows us that powerful brain circuits dedicated to pleasure get triggered when falling in love. The chemical dopamine is released, producing feelings of euphoria and excitement.

Perceiving another person as romantically appealing causes the hypothalamus to transmit chemical messages to the pituitary gland. In turn, the pituitary releases its own hormones into the bloodstream. Nerves around the hypothalamus, *so long as this state of affairs exists for a prolonged time*, produce the blissful biological effect we call "falling in love."

Here's a radical thought... Why do we insist on being in

love only *with someone*? You don't need another person to be in love. Love is not about subject and object. It's a state — a state in which you live.

This becomes especially clear if you've ever lost a lover. The pain is not so much about the loss of the person. We fall in love with being in love, and it's love we miss. Love songs tell us that all the time — and they're right.

Understand this about love, and you'll be moving toward creating the love you need and want. You can bring yourself into the state of love. Love is never about another person. It's about you. You don't really need to have another person to be in love and feel good all the time.

Do this experiment for me. Start professing love to yourself this very minute. And mean it. Just *think* love to yourself! *Feel* it! Hear your inner voice say it! *I love you*. And this, spoken inwardly to yourself: *You ARE Love*. Now... feel the tension go.

Feel your shoulders relax, feel that warmth flow down your back. Feel that unexpected smile come to light up your relaxed face. In just a moment, you feel warm and wonderful. Every cell feels renewed, energized. A blissful feeling washes over and through you. It's just like falling in love.

Your relationships with others are projections of your relationship with yourself. Jealousy, hate, and love are all, ultimately, about you. You're the center of your own reality. You, after all, created that reality. And you're the creator of all the love you'll ever know.

Everyone wants to be in love. So what's stopping you? Begin by giving a few minutes of loving thoughts toward yourself. And you'll be surprised at how much easier it will be for you to love your neighbors.

CHAPTER 30

Know Thyself!

After three years of grueling physical therapy, I remember the day when I was able to stand on my once poorly functioning leg and raise my other leg slightly above my head. I thought I'd experienced how a blind man must have felt when he regained his sight. Exaltation and overflowing gratitude kept me awake until dawn. And on the following morning…

To my total bewilderment, even though I'd kept my gains, the novelty of the lightness was gone and I could no longer sustain the level of elation I felt the day before. I still wanted to voice it, but the desire to shout it had faded. Why? How could the "extraordinary" have become ordinary so quickly?

For fifty years I'd thought, if only I could walk normally—no pain, no discomfort, no worry that people would see my limp—then *nothing* could ever stop me from being truly happy. No. Beyond happy—rapturous…

It always goes like this in our mind: *If only I had…* then

things would be glorious. And, with every rung up the ladder, it was glorious for a day, for fifteen minutes. Then, as B.B. King sings: *The thrill is gone.*

Blessings are not noticeable in their presence, only in their absence. We notice pains, and acknowledge them and do something about them. But health … Well, most of us take it for granted, at least when we have it.

Did you wake up this morning and say thanks that your little toe on your right foot is not hurting? Probably not. It's "normal." Then you stubbed your little toe on the way to the bathroom…Now you can appreciate a healthy toe. But not a moment before.

Also, we don't notice youth, until it's gone. We don't often appreciate those who love us, until they're no longer around.

We believe that celebrities, famous beauties, and rich folks must be much happier than we are. They're not, and for the very same reason. They, just as the rest of us, keep on searching for whatever they don't have.

This made me think. I've long dreamed of doing a real solo dance. I've seen it countless times in my head… swirling joyously as if my body had been perfect from birth. So I'll get there, the moment comes, my first turn, a leap, a twist, the smooth delight of it… *Then* what?

Yes, I expect to feel great joy. I also know that I'll quickly thereafter be asking: Is that all there is? I should have guessed. Millions have absolutely healthy legs, and they don't leap with joy with every step. But this conceptual knowledge doesn't change anything for me. I need this experience, so I'm going for it. It needs to serve its purpose.

Do you harbor wishes for material things—to publish a book, to record an album, to build your own house, to win an Olympic gold medal? Nothing's wrong with that. It merely means you need more experience on the physical level: to be somebody, to have something, to delight in getting it, and experience disappointment when realizing that it doesn't impart lasting satisfaction. It means you need more playing time in this drama called life.

Got a GPS? Even if you don't own a Global Positioning System unit, you know the basic idea. You punch in your destination—123 Main Street, Cleveland, Ohio—and the GPS guides you from backing out of your garage, out onto the highway, onto the right off-ramp in Cleveland, and through the maze of streets to your mother-in-law's house. Miss a turn, take the wrong turn, and your car's GPS will redirect you. "Recalculating," some of them say in a robotic voice.

No matter how far you deviate from your originally programmed route, that GPS and its voice will still be redirecting you back to a better route to your intended destination. Drive halfway to Seattle, and it will still be directing you to Cleveland.

Life has its own GPS, its programmed destination: a spiritual awakening, the realization that separability is an illusion—you and God are one.

We're given choices all the time. But, in the end, they all lead to the same final destination. What we call problems are detours on which life takes us to give us object lessons. Here's a familiar thought: "Whatever doesn't kill me makes me stronger." All experience, in that sense, is good.

Whatever decisions you make, however many delays or

alternative routes you take, however much playtime you allot yourself, that natural and indefeasible navigation system will always be steering you toward self-realization.

Spiritual books teach: You can't satisfy the longings of the spirit with material things. It's not possible to find genuine happiness outside your true spiritual self. The material world will remain an abode of sorrows, pains, and fears, alternating with fleeting pleasures.

Problems indicate a lack of necessary and obtainable self-knowledge. You may think you know yourself, but what you know is what you've learned from others, responding to your physical form. That's why you've become identified with it.

You function as a body, you're viewed as a body, but you are not your body. An identity is a particular point of view from which life is experienced. Each of us experiences infinity — always in momentary glimpses — from a particular perspective, and subject to the qualities we possess. Is each of us only a stack of beliefs, labels, stories, moments, drama, and history that our ego has assembled? There's infinitely more.

Knowing others is wisdom, knowing yourself is Enlightenment.

— Lao-Tzu

The purpose of our earthly existence is to realize who we are: a spiritual being, indestructible, whose nature is Love and whose experience is endless bliss. But it's only when we stop expecting the world to supply us with everlasting joy that we'll be prepared to take the journey inward.

As long as you harbor some longing for worldly achievements — health, beauty, riches, fame, et al — these will tie you to the material world. Their allure will enchain you. To realize that they are worthless, sometimes you must acquire them first. You cannot relinquish, in the end, what you've never had in the first place.

You'll never get past concerns for these material things until you understand them, and understand in particular what they mean for you, how they work in your life. So go ahead: Deal with those material things. Learn to see *into* and *through* them. And someday, you will get beyond them.

If you need to change what you don't like about your life, you can do it. Just as plants turn to the sun, we, too, must turn toward whatever we want, and by giving our attention to it, manifest it into the physical world.

Through solving your problems and constantly expanding your experience in the material world, you'll grow in the understanding of your true nature. Still, at any given moment, *you're perfect the way you are.*

When my friend Scott read this last statement, his remark was: *Aren't you taking this too far? That is not what my bathroom scale is saying.*

One definition of perfect: "… having all the required or desirable elements, qualities, or characteristics; as good as it is possible to be …"

Is a baby of three months any less perfect than a teenager? Those with teenagers are likely to say it's the other way. But consider the parallel case of an apple seed. From germination to full-grown glory, it's perfect at every single moment. Likewise, the infant, the teen, and the grownup are complete human beings, each with endless potential.

At every moment of our life, every one of us is as good as it is possible to be for fulfilling the main purpose of our existence—realizing our unity with God.

Whether a person is a saint in a convent, or a thief on a cross, the possibility of living in a state of Love is always available to him. If he's not ready and needs to grow further, to gain more experience in the physical world, then in the next moment he's still every bit as good for self-realization as he was in the previous moment.

You want to achieve something, not because you're not good enough the way you are, but because growth feels good. You should never resist growth. Stagnation, the cessation of growth, is detrimental not only for a plant, a child, but for you.

Don't look toward the dirt, but don't despise it either. Just as plants need dirt, you need your problems. Yes, you need even your diabetes for something. It's all there for you, all given to you, to assure your evolution and growth.

Ignorance causes suffering. And self-ignorance causes some of the greatest suffering. Knowing the material world is useful for daily living, but it is *self*-knowledge that ends suffering. That is why the wise men of Greece believed that if you "Know Thyself," you will know *everything* and will have found the ultimate path to happiness. Seeing ourselves as alive, vibrating beings is perhaps the most important breakthrough we all have to make.

When the day comes that I dance free from the constraints of my hip injuries, I *believe* at that moment there'll be a big leap in my spiritual development. I'll finally *know* that a physical affliction can only affect my body or my mind, but it can never affect the *real* Me.

Once you have made peace with Higher Self, there is no other peace to seek.

CHAPTER 31

Search For the Heaven Within Us

I'm writing this chapter in the wake of the Germanwings Flight 9525 catastrophe. On March 24, 2015, the plane slammed into a mountainside in the French Alps, killing all 150 people aboard. These 144 passengers and six crewmembers endured eight minutes of rapid descent. At some point during those eight minutes, each person aboard came to know he or she was about to die.

My husband regularly plays table tennis at a nearby church. The day after the crash, a half-hour devotional was held before the table tennis practice. The leader posed a question to the group: *What would YOU do in those eight minutes?* The consensus: You'd need to pray and to proclaim your faith in God, using those minutes to repent, so you could have everlasting life.

Most people might wish they'd use that time in prayer, seeking reconciliation with God and the peace that flows from it. But, overwhelmingly, people experience panic and fear in such moments. Yet, occasionally, there'll be someone who seems completely in the moment, without a sign of worry. Perhaps there was one such person aboard Flight 9525.

Our beliefs influence how we live… and how we die. I want to know what allows a person to be serene and calm in such moments, what lets him defy or ignore the terrifying message of the senses. It turns out it's not so much an intellectual *belief* in God, but an intimate *knowledge* of God that transcends the fear of death.

Much as we try, our minds can never comprehend infinity. So, we can never come to *know* God using the mind. Our rational, finite thinking stands in the way of that comprehension. So we need to get our minds *out* of the way.

According to the University of Southern California's Neuro-Imaging Lab, a person has, on average, 48.6 distinct thoughts per minute.

Let me offer an analogy: We've seen, these past few years, a ten-fold increase in email volume. Imagine all those messages—most of them outright spam—rolling into your inbox at the rate of one per second. And you have to give each at least cursory attention. Overwhelming! But that's how our mind works all day, and often without rest even at night.

Thoughts flow constantly, past to future and back again. You blame yourself for something you did, or fret about something you have to do tomorrow. In your mind, you're endlessly reliving a past that's unfixable, or planning for a future that's unpredictable. Sounds like rather a self-made hell, doesn't it?

Meditation can help. How? Consider it your mental spam filter. Meditation is about seeing what matters to the real, authentic you in the *present* moment. And it's about stripping away the junk.

What does the yogi sitting in his lotus position, Pentecostals speaking in tongues, Dervishes whirling in a dance, and the mystical states of Amerindians have in common? They're all ways of dispelling the illusion of separability. They're about seeking unity with God, with the One, the Universal Spirit, Infinite Love — whichever term best corresponds to their belief system.

Meditation is often linked with the word *prayer*. Prayer and meditation are related, it's true. But they're also quite distinct. Prayer is when you're "talking" to God, while meditation is when you're seeking to "hear" God. As anyone who's meditated can tell you, the mind is the biggest obstacle to "hearing" God.

There are many definitions of meditation. The one I find most helpful: Meditation is a way of getting into the space *between* the thoughts.

Here's a useful analogy from geometry. A line, we all know from high school days, is a continuum. That is to say: Between any two points on that line is an infinite number of other points. Easy proof: Draw a line on paper, left to right. Mark its midpoint. Then, mark the midpoint between that first midpoint and the line's left end. Then mark the middle between *that* midpoint and the left extremity.

On and on we go, and always there's one more "between" we can mark — given a pointy enough pencil! There's no end to it. A line of *any* length — a millimeter, a city block, or the width of the galaxy — contains an infinite number of points. A point is *infinitely small*.

Those spaces between thoughts are pretty small, too, but it's there where infinity lies. Ultimately, it's there that we can discover universal entanglement, enabling us to experience infinity and God.

Over 3,000 scientific studies have been done to prove the benefits of meditation. The list includes claims for every realm of life: Meditation, it seems, increases mental strength and concentration. Improves immune system. Raises energy level. Improves sleep. And even lessens premenstrual and menopausal syndromes. The list of benefits includes just about every physical or mental challenge you might be facing. Here's why...

When we begin to meditate daily, it's like being given access to the energy infinitely bigger than what you sense as the "I", our ego, in the material world. It's there between our thoughts that we find infinite possibility, endless creativity, and solutions to every imaginable problem.

Meditation is the ultimate mobile device; you can use it anywhere, anytime, unobtrusively.

— Sharon Salzberg, *Real Happiness: The Power of Meditation*

There's no need to sit in the lotus position (though it's comfortable). No need for crystal balls or incense or Sri Sri Ravi Shankar recordings. The main thing: For starters, find ten or fifteen minutes a day, and just sit quietly. *Observe* your thoughts. Don't judge. Just let those thoughts float by, whatever they are. If it all seems like spam... fine. Just *be aware*. Just let it pass by in its long parade of supreme irrelevance. I promise you'll appreciate the experience the very first time. But as with every practice, you'll need to do it regularly to get good at it.

Whatever your religious persuasion, whether or not you indeed harbor religious beliefs at all, meditation can help immensely. Buddhists, Hindus, Muslims, even atheists and agnostics, often experience less trouble with meditation than do some Christians.

The difficulty lies in the notion that one must "empty the mind." The worry for some Christians is: If I "empty" my mind, am I not making room for Satan to enter?

What does the meditation practitioner empty the mind *of*? The answer is simple: past and future. What's left? Thoughtless awareness of the present, the immediate moment.

Nor does the meditator lose contact with God in this "emptying." Rather, God is even *more* accessible in the present moment than He is in our endless fretting about past and future. Think about it: Love, death, and meditation have one thing in common: They happen *only* in the present moment.

Through the study of books one seeks God. By meditation one finds Him.

— Padre Pio, Catholic priest

You probably have heard the word *meditation* defined as an especially concentrated form of mental activity. It's a type of "mental exercise" (to borrow one dictionary's phrasing) for the purpose of reaching a heightened level of spiritual awareness — awareness, for example, of God.

But I invite you to think about this: We could hardly comprehend God as infinite through a decidedly finite human mind, could we? Become aware of God, or becoming connected with God, is no mere "mental exercise." Far from mental *activity*, as conventionally understood, what we need is mental *quiet*.

In daily life, our minds are engaged in the petty business of constantly examining and verifying things in the outside world—car payments, kids in school, birds on the lawn. In meditation, though, the mind is turned inward, to become aware of yourself.

When it comes to knowing ourselves, how can we stand in both roles? How can you place yourself in front of yourself? There's a duality intimately wrapped up in all our thinking.

Everything that we say, assert, think, or even ask is filtered through a nearly unavoidable membrane: language. When we talk about self-knowledge, that language issue becomes especially apparent. To know yourself means to become aware of yourself by becoming a witness of yourself. Complicated? It would seem so.

This idea feels quite unnatural, even weird, precisely because language sets us up to see, and to read things, in terms of a self-other, subject-object duality. In deeper states of meditation, there is no longer a subject-object duality to experience, no self-other distinction.

Contemporary philosopher Franklin Merrell-Wolf, in his classic works, *Pathways Through To Space: A Personal Record of Transformation in Consciousness*, describes the state of absolute awareness this way: "In that State where I realize Myself as identical with all space and all objects, there is no division between an 'I' and a 'not-I.' This is equivalent to saying there is but one Element."

Through meditation you can learn that you are spirit, which is indestructible. Once you recognize your—*our*—connectedness with the larger universe in a deeply felt way, you experience a total loving embrace with existence, with God. You *know* what Christ knew: "I and the Father are one." You're experiencing Infinite Love. Could there be any reason for worry—even in extreme circumstances?

Still, many hesitate about "getting into" meditation. I was no exception. It is, for most of us, leaping into the unknown. It's as if we're afraid to experience our own vastness.

I remember the first time I was invited to join a mediation group. I was a church-going person, holding views similar to those of the prayer group Nick was visiting. Oh! How uncomfortable it was for me to see, that first time, people sitting cross-legged, eyes closed, thumb and forefinger connected, hands resting on their knees. It was *alien*. And indeed I thought: *This is un-Christian. What am I doing here?*

But I'm glad I stayed. Glad I figured out meditation is anything but un-Christian, and even gladder that I started to attend a regular meditation class.

It's helped me in many ways. The most important: dealing with fear—specifically, the fear of death. When it comes to meditation, I'm a beginner. Still, I'm looking forward to the day when, on the question, *Do you believe in God?* I could confidently answer the way Carl Jung did: "I don't need to believe. I know."

CHAPTER 32

Love 'em All!

I like to read about the experiences that led people to their achieving spiritual enlightenment. One of these accounts got firmly imprinted on my memory. It's about "Ted," paralyzed from the neck down.

Lying in his hospital bed, bored and depressed, he decided to occupy himself thinking about *pleasant times*. He noticed that when he was reminiscing about his first love, he was reliving those happy moments, and it felt *good*.

Returning to physical reality was always a crushing experience. In the effort to forget his motionless body, he decided to expand the pleasant time by evoking a feeling of love toward every one of his friends. He then extended this feeling to all his acquaintances. Then he would remember his enemies, challenging himself to love them, as well. This felt even better.

Encouraged, Ted started to "generate" love for everyone who walked into his room, then to every piece of furniture, to every tree he could see from his window, and to every leaf on each tree. All of a sudden, his disability ceased to matter. The realization came: He is not his body. He felt one with the doctors, nurses, the hospital, the trees, the whole universe. It felt as if he were merging with *everyone* and *everything*.

Many spiritual texts teach that, once you achieve a state of being in which you realize you are one with the universe, with God, when "your connection to the reality is now permanent and unbreakable," you'll know "an ultimate sense of peace, fulfillment and bliss." And that is how Ted felt from that moment on. Apparently, Ted's extreme circumstances created a situation, aiding him to achieve the state of Infinite Love so few are able to reach.

Love can transport you from the prison of time. We all share a deep longing for love. *That* is why everyone—despite denials—wants to be in love.

Why it is so difficult for us modern humans to love? Part of the answer: *Love is purposeless.* Love is really the most astonishingly absurd pursuit: It has no meaning or purpose beyond itself.

We contemporaries are often remarkably incapable of love. We don't know *how* to love. We cannot really grasp what love *is*.

Consider the biblical viewpoint: *Love is patient, love is kind. It does not envy, it does not boast, it is not proud* … (1 Corinthians 13:4). These beautiful words are standards at most weddings. These *are* qualities of love, and these verses carry a truth and appeal that go beyond the boundaries of any single religious view.

But how does love essentially *feel*? What are love's "symptoms"?

Here are some characteristics of how you feel when experiencing love, as various sages have put it...

- When you are in love, you feel no desire for anything else. You're content, you feel as if you need nothing else.
- You are completely in the present — no focus on the past or the future.
- Your ego fades. *You* are no longer important. Love is the death of your ego.
- When you love, you feel no fear. Not even fear of death. Hence, lovers feel the best time to die is when they are together.

I'll direct your attention, whatever your religious stance may be, to an undeniable symbol of love: Jesus. For Jesus, love was not a mere *relationship*, one individual with another. Rather, it was a state of *being*.

Your romantic love gives you a glimpse of the kind of love Christ intended. Romantic love can become a bridge. When you're in love, your dominion is suddenly changed. You are thrown out of time, and you face eternity. When you are in love, this may be your easiest opportunity, your nearest moment to knowing God, to recognizing your own link with divinity.

When you are in love with your chosen one, then you have in that instant the momentum to love all humanity. Imagine extending this feeling toward your neighbors, and the people you encounter moment by moment in your daily life.

Imagine you are inseparable from each — from your letter carrier, your boss, your server at the restaurant, and the people you have breakfast with in the morning.

Imagine, further, that your own separateness, your "I," is illusory, that all you do for yourself is for them, that all you do for them is for you. Imagine… and that imagining will become real. The world you build as a result would be a lovely place to live.

When you are in love, you cannot hide it—it will show. People in love look differently, walk differently, talk differently. One way to look at enlightenment is falling in love with everyone and everything. That is why an Eastern spiritual master will say to his disciple: *When you become enlightened, don't tell me. I will know.*

So… we're all connected. And what happens to each of us affects the rest of us. Just as all the waters of the world constitute a single ocean, all our individual human spirits collectively are One. We rise and fall, fail and succeed, together.

So you cannot be prosperous without wishing prosperity for others, you cannot be healthy without sharing the secrets of well-being with others, and you cannot get love without giving love to others.

The Scriptures, in Genesis 1: 26-27, emphasize that we are created in the image and likeness of God, our Creator. Because His essence is Love, it is also *our* essence. We have a natural capacity to love. Let's exercise that capacity, just as we exercise our physical bodies. Says 1 John 4:7… "Beloved, let us love one another, for love is of God, and everyone who loves is born of God and knows God."

All religions have similar thoughts about mercy, about kindness. One idea characteristic of Buddhism (though not unique to it), is that our souls come into this life for experiences that will teach us how to love and bring us ever closer to realizing our true nature, which is Love.

Enlightenment, for a wave in the ocean, is the moment the wave realizes it is water.

— Thich Nhat Hanh

Everyone you meet is fighting a battle about which you know nothing. Each of us struggles here on Earth, each in his or her own way, searching out our own path to God. It only makes sense, therefore, to be kind and loving toward our fellow classmates in the school of life.

We are all students, every one of us, in discovering who we really are. A college graduate is no better than a twelfth-grader, or is no better than a first-grader. Some just need more time and effort to learn than others.

How can you love a person who's done something terrible? How could Jesus love and forgive the thief on the cross? Only by seeing others as children of God — extensions of God, imprisoned by their senses. Their dis-eased minds created an illusion of separability, when only Oneness is real.

The Sanskrit word for enlightenment is *bodhi*, which means "awakened." This can be defined as an awakening to a great reality which most of us never perceive. (Remember: Quantum theory reveals that what we do perceive isn't real.) This level of understanding is a high bar, and few ever reach it.

What happened for Ted is a possibility that exists within all of us. Ted's story teaches us that no problem in life should be labeled as "bad."

Even when you find yourself in a situation when there is no hope left in the physical world, *then*, just like Ted, you might be closer to awakening to the true reality and experiencing pure bliss more than the rest of humanity. And, depending upon your religious preference, *that is* how you find God, or achieve enlightenment.

I started this book with this one principal premise: To achieve anything of material worth, you need to separate yourself from the crowd. Do what so few are doing: become powerful beyond measure and manifest into physical reality anything you can envision for yourself.

But once you've achieved health, riches, fame, and whatever else the physical realm can offer, you'll sooner or later realize this... Nothing material can bring lasting happiness.

Nothing *outside* you is worth having. The only thing worth having, ultimately, lies within. And what is that? It's achieving the state of love, which is realizing our true nature. Love your neighbour. Love 'em All! Because to merge with God, with Infinite Love, we cannot have any feeling toward ourselves or others that is not loving.

Conclusion

I s there a *key*, indeed, to transcending personal problems? Yes. It's profoundly simple: It's the realization that there is, ultimately, no separation between you and Infinite Love. However, simple doesn't mean easy.

In fact, very few people have ever achieved a state of *perfect* awareness of quantum nonseparability. We may live a lifetime before ever meeting such a person. But that shouldn't stop us from searching for such individuals, who, in an enlightened way, have touched oneness with the whole of humanity and the universe.

Reading Socrates, Spinoza, Whitman, Thoreau, Franklin Merrell-Wolf and others who have written about cosmic consciousness can help us to understand — roughly, vaguely — where the path leads.

I'm only at the very beginning of that path of self-discovery, making my first exploratory steps. Most of you are probably beginners too. Nevertheless, we can all "get" the notion of nonseparability. Get it, that is, intellectually, in the same way we grasp that the Earth is round, or that electricity exists and flows through the wires in our houses.

It's likely, that none of us have done all the experiments or made the direct observations that prove these facts. But we have some book learning, or some personal experiences that help us know.

What you know about electricity stops you from deliberately touching live AC wires. What you know about gravity prevents you from walking off cliffs. Why not gain that kind of knowledge about nonseparability?

Read popular books on quantum mechanics. Watch YouTube videos on the topic. Keep going at it until you're convinced. Remind yourself of it again and again. Find facts in support of this quantum phenomena.

Your belief in nonseparability, your understanding the universal law *What you have believed will be done for you*—once you have fully accepted these concepts—will make you the master of your life.

The other day, a relative asked me: How's life? I thought of the perfect answer: *Life's marvelous! It always looks after you, if you let it.* However, I didn't say that. Minutes before, he was complaining about his life. This relative of mine *makes* his life hard.

His perpetual grumpiness, his negative take on *everything*, gives him the very kind of life he complains about. We're all constantly creating our lives. And he's dedicated to making his hard. It doesn't have to be that way.

Healthy? Happy? Free? Can you really be these things? You *can*. Stop lugging your problems around like dead weight. Make *them* carry *you*. Life's trials are there to lift you up—not drag you down. Don't carry them on your shoulders. Use them like stepping stones to help you to the pinnacle of your life.

Though the challenge you're facing might be a real beast, there *is* purpose in it. There's value, too. The issue itself is never quite as bad as it looks. Life is leading you to something better. *Step here*, life says. *It's safe.* And life will grant you that safety, painlessly—unless you're kicking and resisting with all your might.

Life's trials are given us for a purpose, for our growth, to teach us to trust life. Be receptive to the possibilities that each new situation—even a conflict—may hand you. Let your life take a different shape, the way water takes the shape of its container, never insisting on your own predetermined mold. Be assertive, but never resentful.

Life… is flux. Life… is constant change. A problem *arises*, and *stays* a problem, precisely when and where you resist the change… when you resist life itself. Change, the only constant, is good. Change is what living is all about.

The bigger the problem, the more you'll need to change. A big problem is a call to a broader perspective on life, an invitation to experience life from different points of view—sometimes radically different, sometimes subtly so. By searching for a solution, never stopping until you find it, you'll transform your life.

I hope reading this book has changed your outlook. I hope you'll never again think of life as "hard." If you think life is inherently, necessarily hard… it will be. In contrast, if you live a life that allows bright sunlight to fall on every scene, if you believe in the power of possibility, if you believe deeply in the connectedness of all things, all people… you *can* lead the life you want—the life of your dreams.

Ultimately, life's trials are there to teach us to love. When we're in love we feel we can do *anything*. It's because when we are in a state of love, we feel closest to God, the creator. Think of it as "vibrating on God's frequency," where everything is possible.

If you want something in life, create it: Get into a loving and genuinely grateful state. Get grateful, indeed for the very thing you're wishing, as if you already have it. Live in a state of love and gratitude, and there's no limit to your creative power.

You've finished reading the book. Or not. In fact, I hope not. I've packed a lot of ideas into each chapter. Sometimes a bit too much, in hopes you'd return and read the whole book, and its individual chapters, again and again.

Our senses, our egos are always at work, building and rebuilding the illusion of separation, making us small and fearful of outside circumstances. Therefore, we need to be reminded daily of our oneness with God, reminded of our true reality and how our emotions become the fuel of creation for the life we live.

The book is finished. But I hope a new, upward spiral curve of your own self-discovery has just begun.

Your Right to Be Beautiful: The Miracle of Raw Foods

2004 ForeWord magazine Health Book of the Year Award finalist.

Learn to build a lifestyle that can take you to the pinnacle of health and beauty. Your Right To Be Beautiful shows you how to cultivate your natural beauty — without expensive products, cosmetic surgery, or advice from pricey consultants.

ISBN 978-0-97424344-3 • paperback • 346 pages

Rawsome Flex: Beautifying System of Facial Exercises and Raw Foods

Imagine a rubber band — permanently stretched. That's a good image of the way muscles may have weakened, lengthened, and drooped in your face. You can shorten those flabby muscles through facial exercises that lift and firm your face. Rawsome Flex's 30 exercises, with illustrations and detailed instructions, will help you, in just 21 days, to make a permanent change for the better.

ISBN 978-0-97424347-4 • paperback • 128 pages

Quantum Eating: The Ultimate Elixir of Youth

Quantum Eating is the gate to health and longevity. Questions about aging, quandaries which have baffled experts for centuries, get answered in clear, straight talk. This truly mind-energizing book brims with fresh insights that challenge our most basic assumptions. Here are ready-to-use secrets to help you achieve superior health and youthful glow, and avoid the unattractiveness of aging.

ISBN 978-097424341-2 • paperback • 450 pages

Guide to an Ageless Face: The Smartest Skin Training System

Your skin has a remarkable ability to rejuvenate itself. Mainstream "experts" don't use this ability enough. That's why many people get desperate — they opt for expensive, dangerous surgery and skin-filler procedures. There is a better way. Here's a revolutionary "Skin Training System" that will train your face to replace old cells with new ones with youthful regularity and bring on that glow, without sacrificing health for beauty.

E-book • 82 pages

The Raw Food Diet and Your Compromised Teeth

What will happen to your fillings when you go on a raw food diet? How much bleaching can your teeth take? What should you know about mercury amalgam fillings…root canals…titanium implants? Can a raw food regimen "cure" an abscess? How can you prevent your teeth from going bad in the future? Here's a complete guide for people leading raw or near-raw lifestyles, with answers you can't get anywhere else!

E-book • 130 pages

100 Days to 100% Raw: A Step by Step Guide

Here's a dynamic, step-by-step curriculum, teaching the fundamentals of the raw food lifestyle. These do-it-yourself steps will kick-start your health and improve your looks, whether you're a first-timer or well on your way. Tips from real-life experience will have you stepping faster and more surely along your own road to vastly improved health and looks.

E-book • 120 pages